ARREST
OF SHIPS

ARREST OF SHIPS

By

CHRISTOPHER HILL
M.A.(Oxon.), F.I.C.S.

KAY SOEHRING
Hamburg

TAMEYUKI HOSOI
Tokyo

CHRISTIE HELMER
Portland, Oregon

LONDON   NEW YORK   HAMBURG   HONG KONG

LLOYD'S OF LONDON PRESS LTD.

1985

Lloyd's of London Press Ltd.
Legal Publishing and Conferences Division
26–30 Artillery Lane, London E1 7LX

U.S.A. AND CANADA
Lloyd's of London Press Inc.
87 Terminal Drive, Plainview
New York, NY 10003 U.S.A.

GERMANY
Lloyd's of London Press
PO Box 11 23 47, Deichstrasse 41
2000 Hamburg 11, West Germany

SOUTH EAST ASIA
Lloyd's of London Press (Far East) Ltd.
1502 Chung Nam Building
1 Lockhart Road, Wanchai
Hong Kong

©

Christopher Hill, Kay Soehring,
Tameyuki Hosoi, Christie Helmer
1985

British Library Cataloguing in Publication Data
Arrest of ships.
1. Arrest of ships
I. Hill, Christopher
342.3'965   K1188.A7

ISBN 1–85044–025–5

Printed in Great Britain by
The Eastern Press Ltd.
London and Reading

Foreword

There is, perhaps, a considerable measure of misunderstanding of the extent of uniformity internationally about the rules for ship arrest. It is not as uniform as people tend to imagine. The misconception is probably fuelled by the existence of the International Convention on the Arrest of Sea-going Ships of 1952. The number of sovereign States which adopted it into their own domestic legal systems is severely limited, however. Because of this, the "64,000 dollar" question which your hypothetical bona fide maritime claimant will likely pose is – "where, how and when can I most advantageously arrest a ship in pursuit of my particular claim?". Such a question is virtually incapable of helpful and definitive answer. The contributors to this volume hope that they have at least made a start.

The primary purpose of this work is to acquaint all those who may ever have occasion to take arrest action, because of some grievance they may have, with the law, practice and procedure of arrest of vessels. Four countries have been selected and offered as comparative examples of what does happen. Basically this is not a law book exclusively, nor is it exclusively a book of practice; it is, so the contributors hope, a book combining both aimed at enlightening the knowledge of those with little experience in this field and also of refreshing the minds of those who may already be familiar on both sides (plaintiff and shipowner defendant and their respective counsellors alike) with an up-to-date summary of the law and practice.

One main aim of the 1952 Convention was to restrict the number and type of claims for which a vessel could be arrested (some 17 types). The claims must have a connection with the operation of a ship. One distinct and basic feature of the Convention is the absence from it of an international law of arrest. The law and procedural rules applicable is/are those of the forum within which any particular arrest takes place.

Being a contracting State to a Convention involves a contractual duty on each signatory State (once the minimum number of States have signified acceptance as required by the Convention itself) to "put its act together" (if readers will pardon the pun), i.e. to implement and/or enact the provisions of the Convention into its domestic legislation.

The Arrest Convention itself does not "speak" in terms of liability *in personam* either in respect of the involved ship at the time of the incident which gave rise to the claim or in respect of any other potentially "arrestable" ship at the time when the arrest action is brought. The Convention itself does not concern itself with the matter of jurisdiction to consider the merits of the claim itself.

The four countries featured in this book are selected for no specific reason other than perhaps the following: England (and Wales) because of its long standing maritime tradition and the frequency of the use of its courts by foreigners worldwide; the United States for the same reasons and because of the massiveness of its coastline and the geographical likelihood of vessel arrests being made within the jurisdiction of its courts; West Germany as an example of a leading West European maritime nation; and Japan as a powerful example of a maritime nation in the Orient. One factor which did perhaps influence the choice of these particular four was that two of them have adopted the 1952 Arrest Convention (England and West Germany) and two have not (United States and Japan).

The reader is at liberty to decide for himself as to whether he wishes to regard this work as a comparative study or not.

It is the belief of the co-authors that although there have been numerous articles published over the years with varying degrees of academic brilliance and also there have been "heavy" and indeed very "light" books covering the subject, this is the first volume to be published giving a medium-depth insight into this useful, controversial and internationally-focused subject. It is the hope of the co-authors and publisher that this will be the first in a series of volumes summarizing the law and procedure of ship arrest in many different countries.

There is no ready answer, as has been said, to the question "which is the best jurisdiction in which to arrest a ship?" Everything depends naturally on the factors of each individual case. "Forum shopping" is an activity (cynics would call it a sport) which has been commonly practised by maritime claimants the world over. The intention of this work is to assist people to have a greater awareness of their rights and of the options which are available to them in exercising those rights. It is not intended to answer the question for them but to make it easier for them to answer it for themselves.

I would like to express my sincere thanks to Mr. J. A. Schofield and Mr. H. Kesweni who kindly devoted of their time to look over the draft of my section on England and Wales.

CHRISTOPHER HILL

Contents

THE FEDERAL REPUBLIC OF GERMANY

JAPAN

The Authors

CHRISTOPHER HILL was born in 1932. After two years' compulsory military service in the early 1950s he studied law at Oxford University and obtained an honours degree. Thereafter he spent three years working in operational shipping for the Swire Group in Hong Kong and subsequently six years working for a leading firm of shipping agents in the Arabian Gulf. Since 1966 he has been working for the managers of an old-established P & I Club.

He lectures part-time in shipping law at the City of London Polytechnic and the London School of Foreign Trade and for five years in the late 1970s he lectured also to post-graduate students at University College London. He writes legal comments regularly for the *Shipbroker* and *Seatrade* journals and is the author of *An Introduction to the Law of Carriage of Goods by Sea* (Stanford Maritime) and *Maritime Law* (Lloyd's of London Press), the second edition of which will be published in mid-1985. He is a Fellow of the Institute of Chartered Shipbrokers and an Associate of the Institute of Arbitrators.

KAY SOEHRING is 45 and a lawyer in Hamburg. He became Doctor of Laws (Dr. Jur.) in 1967 and was admitted to the local bar in 1969 after employment with a major German bank. He has been a partner of Westphal & Voges, Hamburg, since 1970, and is an expert in the international aspects of civil procedure, including arbitration, maritime, banking, bankruptcy and other fields of business law.

TAMEYUKI HOSOI was born at Shizuoka-Ken (Japan) in 1943 and educated at the Faculty of Law, Chuo University of Tokyo (LL.B., 1966); Legal Training and Research Institute of the Supreme Court of Tokyo (1970–72); and University College London (Diploma in Shipping Law, 1977). He was associate lawyer with the Braun Moriya Hoashi & Kubota law firm of Tokyo (1972–79); visiting lawyer with the Lillick McHose & Charles law firm of San Francisco (1978); and is now a partner of the Hiratsuka & Partners law firm of Tokyo (1979).

Tameyuki Hosoi is a member of the First Tokyo Bar Association (1972); a member of the Business Law Section of the International Bar Association (1978); and of the Japanese Maritime Law Academy (1981). He has been an overseas correspondent for *Lloyd's Maritime and Commercial Law Quarterly* since 1982.

CHRISTIE HELMER has been admitted to practise before the Oregon State Courts and the Federal United States Supreme Court, the Ninth Circuit Court of Appeals and the United States District Court for the District of

Oregon since 1974. She is a member of the Maritime Law Association of the United States and was honoured by the Federal Court judges in 1984 by being selected as a lawyer delegate to the Ninth Circuit Judicial Conference. Mrs. Helmer is currently a member of the steering committee for the Pacific Northwest Admiralty Institute and recently completed a three-year term on the Oregon State Bar Board of Governors, an elected office. Mrs. Helmer is a frequent speaker at admiralty conferences on a variety of topics in admiralty law and practice.

Table of Cases

Table of Legislation

UNITED STATES

England and Wales

CHRISTOPHER HILL

The right to arrest a ship is part of the law of England and is recognized by international Convention. It is a valuable weapon in the hands of any court exercising Admiralty jurisdiction. All ship-owners are or should be aware of it. (Sheen, J., in *The Helene Roth*[1].) To gain an understanding of the law of arrest prevailing in England and Wales it must be borne in mind that Britain is a common law country and that Admiralty law has been superimposed over the years by various statutory enactments from time to time. The legal ability to seize a vessel by legal process is therefore partly based on rights conferred by general maritime law and partly upon the right to take legal action of this nature granted by statute. It is the object of this section of this work to enlighten the reader as to how, when, why and in what circumstances arrest may take place and what, roughly, it will cost the arresting party in terms of money and effort.

Historical summary

Admiralty Court Acts in the 19th century (1840 and 1861) gave birth in English law to the statutory right to arrest, originally conferring it upon claimants in respect of necessary materials supplied or services rendered (such as towage) to foreign vessels. *In rem* jurisdiction was expanded in 1873–75 by the Supreme Court of Judicature Acts of those years and the right was next crystallized by the Supreme Court of Judicature (Consolidation) Act 1925. This was eventually replaced by the Administration of Justice Act 1956, itself being "ousted" by the Supreme Court Act 1981.

The 1956 statute was Britain's attempt to adopt the International Convention on the Arrest of Sea-going Ships 1952. Much of shipping law is based on international Convention (excellent in the interests of uniformity) and after the Second World War this Arrest Convention was a significant development. As will be seen later, however, Britain's 1956 statute was a somewhat half-hearted attempt to adopt the Convention and caused dilemmas and endless need for judicial

1. *The Helene Roth* [1980] 1 Lloyd's Rep. 477.

1

interpretation, incident by incident, which only in the year 1982 became resolved by amending legislation (the 1981 statute). *But*, so as immediately to qualify the preceding comment, it should be emphasized that the 1952 Convention has *not* created an international *law* of arrest. That was never the intention of the Convention itself, which was to leave the law governing the arrest of any particular ship to that country where the arrest actually takes place.

The maritime lien – what is it?

As already mentioned, English law must be looked at from two different aspects because England's maritime law is founded on the general maritime law of the land and also upon statutory law. The *maritime lien* is a right which springs from general maritime law and is based on the concept that the ship (personified) has *itself* caused harm, loss or damage to others or to their property and must *itself* make good that loss. The ship is, in other words, the wrongdoer, not its owners. This is, to the realist, a nonsense. How can a hunk of metal do wrong? But it *is* the instrumentality by which its owners or their legal servants do wrong. One of the best and oldest examples of a maritime lien is that arising as a result of a collision at sea. At the moment of impact and the consequential causing of harm to others or to their property a maritime lien arises in favour of all those thus suffering, attaching to the ship (as it were a leech to human skin). The right is, however, inchoate and of "paper" value only until it is put into effect by legal process through the medium of the Admiralty Court. It is in this practical aspect of enforcement where the general maritime law, which incorporates this right of lien, runs on parallel lines to the sophisticated statutory right to arrest which is available under English statutory law in certain defined situations and to a statutorily-stated list of maritime claimants (as will be explained later on).

Who has a maritime lien – ranking for priority

In addition to maritime claimants after a collision, English law confers a lien on other categories of claimant (a privileged few) namely unpaid wages claimants (crew); a *master* for his disbursements (interestingly this lien is conferred by statute (the Merchant Shipping

Act 1970, section 18), and not by the ordinary law) and salvage (reward) claimants. There are others[2] but collision, salvage and wage claimants are the three major commercial categories. The origin of a salvage lien was possessory originally, i.e. a common law possessory lien. This became inconvenient so the nature of the lien was changed to maritime. The lien, being attached to the ship, survives through subsequent changes of ownership until it merges with a judgment in favour of the claimant or is destroyed by neglect to enforce it (laches) or the claim is fully satisfied short of legal proceedings.

A maritime lien in English law has been defined by textbook writers in two ways either as (i) a privileged claim against a ship to be put into effect by legal process, or (ii) a right to a part of the property in the *res* (the ship). The essence of a maritime lien was expressed concisely by the court in *The Bold Buccleugh*[3] as a right which "travels" with the ship into whose possession it may go subsequently. In hindsight the judge in that case might have extended this slightly by saying "and *where*soever it and that subsequent possession may be". Because it, the ship, is to "pay for the wrong it has done" it must be compelled to do so by Admiralty process by forced sale, thus making the proceeds of sale available to satisfy the existing lien holders; if the proceeds are limited then each privileged creditor will receive satisfaction in a court-determined order of priorities until the available proceeds are exhausted. The buyer of the vessel in an *Admiralty* sale acquires a *clean*, unencumbered title. Maritime liens must necessarily be given each a priority rating because of the likelihood that when a ship is sold by Admiralty Court order for the purpose of satisfying not only the lien holders as privileged claimants but others less privileged (for example, registered, or even unregistered, mortgagees, those with mere rights *in rem* and indeed possibly almost anybody – namely judgment debtors, trustees in bankruptcy) there will be limited proceeds only. The distribution of the proceeds is not similar to a *limitation* fund – shared out on a pro rata basis – but each creditor is carefully and painstakingly ranked. The general system of ranking (though the courts have discretion to vary this if equitable principles

2. Other maritime liens recognized by English law: a. Bottomry (now virtually obsolete); b. Fees and expenses of Receiver of Wreck (but this is the product of statute – Merchant Shipping Act 1894, section 567(2) – rather than general maritime law; c. Remuneration to coastguards in respect of services rendered to shipwrecked property, again statutory in origin (Merchant Shipping Act 1894, section 568(1). Both these latter two liens could be reasonably described as "quasi" maritime liens.

3. *The Bold Buccleugh* (1851) 7 Moo. P.C. 267.

and natural justice so dictate in any given situation) is that a *salvor's* lien ranks first, and if more than one salvor, the later before the earlier. The salvor obtains such a high priority because without the emergency services he renders there would be no funds or proceeds preserved for anybody at all to be satisfied.

After salvors come the so-called "damage" liens, those claimants who have suffered as a result of a ship having itself done damage, e.g. ship-to-ship collision or a vessel colliding with a fixed object. These people are innocent sufferers and thus are deserving of a reasonably high priority in ranking. There is probably also an element of encouragement or warning to shipowners and their masters that they should "drive carefully" when navigating their vessel during day-to-day operations.

Next, and last, of the lien holders come the so-called "contractual" liens – bottomry bond holders (this system is now virtually obsolete in these days of highly sophisticated extending of credit) or masters' and crews' unpaid wages. These liens are founded upon contractual breaches (of a contract of employment) and thus the claimant is unable to argue morally that he is an "innocent sufferer". He is deemed to have entered into the contract originally with his eyes open knowing that such a misfortune might well befall him, human nature being what it is.

Why, some might well ask, are salvors' liens not contractual in nature and therefore not ranked below, say, damage liens? Apart from the reasons given above for their top-ranking priority, it should be said that they are classed as "quasi-contractual" so far as academic classification is concerned. Salvors' services are rendered voluntarily, not as a result of a contractual duty but in situations of danger and emergency and where necessary to preserve maritime property. This, despite the likely signing of a salvage agreement, ensures their status as highest ranking.

How do maritime liens relate in the "ranking ladder" to mortgages? Generally, maritime liens enjoy precedence, whether the mortgage be registered or unregistered. Mortgagees enjoy, under English law, a special category status.

One very frequently occurring priority rivalry against proceeds of the *res* is that of mortgagee on the one hand and "necessaries" man on the other. The argument that "necessaries" men should have the same supporting argument in their favour as salvors, that they "help to preserve the *res*", does not avail them. They, so far as English legal opinion goes, rank below mortgagees who, although their claim is really in substance no "more nor less" than his whose claim carries a right *in rem* only (e.g. cargo owners for loss or damage to their property, bunker suppliers, pilotage or towage claimants) are accorded a special status in English law – fitting neatly between maritime liens and what some textbook writers call (wrongly, I believe) statutory liens.

A shiprepairer's lien

The special status of a shiprepairer is worth comment. He has two rights: (i) a possessory lien which is a product of the common law, and (ii) a right to proceed *in rem* against the ship.

His possessory lien, if he exercises it, is subordinate to any maritime liens which may have accrued against the ship earlier, for example master's or crew's wages overdue at the time the possessory lien is exercised. If he forgoes his possessory lien by losing physical possession of the ship and leaves himself merely his right to proceed *in rem* against the ship, he may find himself worse off in the order of priorities.

Lack of international consensus produces conflict of laws

The lack of international uniformity on the subject of priorities in competing maritime claims against the same *res* serves only to encourage "forum shopping". A claimant may think he has a valuable right according to his own national law, but if he finds himself in the hands of a court competent to determine priorities in some foreign jurisdiction and that court considers that the claim is less relatively valuable than the claimant had assumed, the claimant may lose if the liquidated *res* proves a meagre treasure house.

It is of prime importance that some form of international agreement is reached regarding (i) what categories of claim carry a maritime lien; and (ii) how they rank for priority if the ship which is the object of the lien does not realize a sufficient fund to pay off all lienors in full.

Problems arising from jurisdictional conflict

It is a fundamental and essential function of an English Admiralty

Court to assist creditors to obtain satisfaction of their *just* claims. This function, which expresses itself by the giving of effect to a maritime lien, is of an *executive* nature. By arresting and selling the ship the court creates the fund out of which privileged creditors may be satisfied, subject to the system of priorities (mentioned earlier) which may rank one in front of another in the event that full satisfaction to each is impossible.

A maritime lien is a *proprietary* interest in the property; it subtracts from the absolute title of the owner. English jurists in the past have disagreed among themselves as to whether it is truly a right *in* the property (a *jus in re*) or a right *against* the property (a *jus in rem*) only. The logical explanation is that the lien is *both*, a right in the property perfected by action (*in rem*) against it.

A problem which has exercised the minds of practitioners and academics alike is the question of whether maritime liens, recognized as a created right inherent in the claim by a *foreign* system of law, should be recognized *at the time of enforcement* by an English court bringing it into effect against the object of the lien – the vessel. Furthermore, where there is a need to determine priorities among lien holders whose liens attach to the proceeds of that same vessel sold to satisfy them, should the order of priorities be determined according to the law of the country where the lien was created (*lex loci*) or the law of the country exercising jurisdiction (*lex fori*)?

The problem received a definitive judicial pronouncement in *The Halcyon Isle* case.[4] The Privy Council was considering an appeal to it from a Singapore court. They decided that the consensus of English case-law authority concluded that liens are enforceable in actions *in rem* in English courts where *and only where* the events on which the claim is founded would have given rise to a maritime lien in English law if those events had occurred within the territorial jurisdiction of the English court. This was a majority decision (3–2). The majority acknowledged that a maritime lien followed the property through changes of ownership and was enforceable against an innocent purchaser, but nevertheless refused to define the lien as more than remedial and procedural. The question of priorities *was* purely jurisdictional and should be a matter for determination exclusively by the *lex fori*. The minority refused to accept this view, maintaining that a maritime lien is a right of property and that that was the original concept of a lien of this sort and was in keeping with the principles of

4. *The Halcyon Isle* [1981] A.C. 221.

the law of the sea. With this latter view the writer agrees. Certain claims carry a lien, the lien travels with the ship and it would be a denial of this simple principle to say that the recognition and priority bestowed upon it were exclusively for the determination of the eventual *lex fori*. With *priorities* the procedural theory is *admittedly* logical and with the creation or nature of the lien the jurisdictional theory is logical as a prevailing determinator *if* there are several liens from various countries attaching to the same vessel. But what seems utterly irreconcilable is the premise that a right in the nature of a proprietary interest is nevertheless only a procedural or remedial right. *The Halcyon Isle* case does nothing to resolve or even clarify the question of how a conflict of laws should treat liens. The answer is that both views, majority and minority, have their flaws. For an English court to refuse to recognize foreign legal thinking on the nature and creation of a lien is to deny the reasonably smooth "dovetailing" process of the conflict of laws, but, on the other hand, a forum should not be obliged to recognize a foreign right if it is against its established principles to do so.

Need for international uniformity

The foregoing adds fuel to the plea that there should be a much wider adoption of international Conventions on the subject of maritime liens and mortgages so as to unify not only the varied individual national thinking on which claims confer maritime liens and which do not but also the question of ranking of priorities as between maritime lien holders, mortgagees and other creditors.

A purchaser of a ship always has to reckon with the possibility of maritime liens and under many foreign laws all or most of the claims which, in England, only give a right of action *in rem* give rise to such liens (Sheen, J., in *The Helene Roth*).

How may a maritime lien be extinguished by lapse of time?

It can. The original and traditional method of extinction was the application of the doctrine of laches – the idea that if the lien holder "slept" on his right and neglected to pursue it for an unreasonable time then he should lose the right. This idea was coupled with the notion that such neglectful delay would have seriously prejudiced the interests of the defendant potentially responsible. As to what constitutes delay of a length so unreasonable as to persuade a court to discharge the lien depends upon the judge's discretion. A clearly influencing factor will be whether the object of the lien has already passed into the hands of an innocent purchaser or whether it still remains in the hands of the original owner who would be liable. In the former event, delay will be likely to be considered as much *less* excusable.

In the course of his judgment in one of the very rare examples in modern times of laches being pleaded as a counter to the enforcement of a maritime lien (*The Alletta*[5]) Mocatta, J., quoted an old mid-19th century judicial ruling (extracted from *The Bold Buccleugh*[6]) as follows:

It is not necessary to say that the lien is indelible, and may not be lost by negligence or delay where the rights of third parties may be compromised; but where reasonable diligence is used, and the proceedings are laid in good faith, the lien may be enforced, in whosesoever possession the thing may come.

Mocatta, J., had no recent sources at all to call on; he had only 19th century precedents, another of which was an extract from an 1891 case (*The Kong Magnus*[7]):

There are no decisions which enable me to fix any particular period in relation to laches, and I come to the conclusion that the principle that should guide my decision is this, that in each case it is necessary to look at the particular circumstances, and see whether it would be inequitable, after the period of time, which of course is taken into account, and after the circumstances which may have happened (including amongst those the loss of witnesses, the loss of evidence, and including also the change of property), to entertain a suit of this kind.

It would be fair to say that the *practical* application of a laches defence in modern-day English courts has virtually disappeared and has become more of an academic collector's item. It has been superseded over the 80 years of this century gradually by various statutory time limitation periods from time to time. Laches is, however, still to be found frequently pleaded in United States courts.

To take each category of commercial claimant in turn, the limitation periods are:

(a) Salvage. The period is statutorily laid down in section 8 of the

5. *The Alletta* [1974] 1 Lloyd's Rep. 40.
6. (1851) 7 Moo. P.C. 267.
7. *The Kong Magnus* [1891] P. 223.

Maritime Conventions Act 1911 (the United Kingdom's adoption of the Collision and Salvage Convention 1910) – two years from the date when salvage services were rendered. The court may extend the period at its discretion if it thinks fit and considers that there has been no reasonable opportunity to arrest the ship (or other *res*).

(b) Collision claims. Also two years under the same section of the same Act, also extendable at the court's discretion. This will include not only property loss or damage claims but also death or injury, but it should be emphasized that the 1911 statute is contemplating claims brought either by one ship against the other or others *or* by third parties against the *other* ship(s) in the collision. Thus, for example, if passenger ship A collides with ship B and ship B is at least partly to blame, injured passenger X on ship A must bring any action he intends to against ship *B* within two years from the date of the collision (under section 8 of the 1911 statute). If he brings a claim against the ship on which he was actually travelling (ship A), assuming it was at least partly to blame, then the question of whether his claim is time barred will be governed by the terms of his passage contract or any law controlling the contractual terms and conditions (see, for example, the Athens Convention which now has the force of law in England by virtue of the Merchant Shipping Act 1979).

Other personal injury or death claims (excluding those brought under the Maritime Conventions Act, as mentioned above) are controlled as to time lapse by the Limitation Act 1980, which provides for a *three*-year period.

Statutory rights "in rem"

Maritime lienors are, under English law, a privileged few. What of the vast bulk of maritime claimants, the cargo owner whose goods are damaged through bad stowage, the stevedore who is injured when a ship's boom drops on him, the bunker supplier whose bill remains unpaid for an unreasonable length of time? How, when, why and where can they take arrest action? This is where English law provides *statutory* remedies – the action *in rem*. English legal theory has almost universally accepted the procedural theory of action *in rem*, i.e. to secure the defendant owner's personal appearance to court action. Action *in rem* should itself be distinguished from "maritime attachment". In a nutshell, the latter is directed against the *person* whereas the former is directed against the *ship* (or other *res*). The United Kingdom, by the Administration of Justice Act 1956 (Part I) adopted, if somewhat "scratchily", the 1952 Arrest Convention and for the first time in its legal history introduced within its legal system a facility for the judicial arrest not only of the offending or involved ship in a maritime incident (irrespective of where in the world the incident may have taken place) resulting in loss, damage, or harm, but also a ship under the same beneficial ownership as that ship.

Types of claim which give the claimant a right "in rem"

To turn therefore to statutory rights *in rem*, we enter the realm now of Admiralty Court jurisdiction. The word "jurisdiction" merely means the "power" of a court to hear and determine certain types of dispute or claim. What types of claim or dispute are in the power of the English Admiralty Court to hear and determine are set out and defined in a list which may be found written in section 20(2) of the Supreme Court Act 1981. It is appropriate here to quote that subsection in full:

20.–(2) The questions and claims referred to in subsection (1)(a) are—
  (*a*) any claim to the possession or ownership of a ship or to the ownership of any share therein;
  (*b*) any question arising between the co-owners of a ship as to possession, employment or earnings of that ship;
  (*c*) any claim in respect of a mortgage of or charge on a ship or any share therein;
  (*d*) any claim for damage received by a ship;
  (*e*) any claim for damage done by a ship;
  (*f*) any claim for loss of life or personal injury sustained in consequence of any defect in a ship or in her apparel or equipment, or in consequence of the wrongful act, neglect or default of—
    (i) the owners, charterers or persons in possession or control of a ship; or
    (ii) the master or crew of a ship, or any other person for whose wrongful acts, neglects or defaults the owners, charterers or persons in possession or control of a ship are responsible, being an act, neglect or default in the navigation or management of the ship, in the loading, carriage or discharge of goods on, in or from the ship, or in the embarkation, carriage or disembarkation of persons on, in or from the ship;
  (*g*) any claim for loss of or damage to goods carried in a ship;

(*h*) any claim arising out of any agreement relating to the carriage of goods in a ship or to the use or hire of a ship;

(*j*) any claim in the nature of salvage (including any claim arising by virtue of the application, by or under section 51 of the Civil Aviation Act 1949, of the law relating to salvage to aircraft and their apparel and cargo);

(*k*) any claim in the nature of towage in respect of a ship or an aircraft;

(*l*) any claim in the nature of pilotage in respect of a ship or an aircraft;

(*m*) any claim in respect of goods or materials supplied to a ship for her operation or maintenance;

(*n*) any claim in respect of the construction, repair or equipment of a ship or in respect of dock charges or dues;

(*o*) any claim by a master or member of the crew of a ship for wages (including any sum allotted out of wages or adjudged by a superintendent to be due by way of wages);

(*p*) any claim by a master, shipper, charterer or agent in respect of disbursements made on account of a ship;

(*q*) any claim arising out of an act which is or is claimed to be a general average act;

(*r*) any claim arising out of bottomry;

(*s*) any claim for the forfeiture of condemnation of a ship or of goods which are being or have been carried, or have been attempted to be carried, in a ship, or for the restoration of a ship or any such goods after seizure, or for droits of Admiralty.

Of this list the one claim which has probably attracted the most controversy is that under subparagraph (*h*). In *The Eschersheim*[8] the taking of *in rem* arrest action against a tug under common ownership with a salvage tug which had performed abortive salvage services after a collision between two ocean vessels (the failure of the salvage operation being due to the negligence of the tug master and crew) was upheld as valid by the House of Lords as falling within subpara. (*h*). The hire of the tug was considered to be directly pursuant to an agreement for the use or hire of a ship.

Further illustrative of the correct construction of this subpara. was the 1984 case of *The Antonis P. Lemos*.[9] Here the claim endorsed on the writ *in rem* was a simple claim for damages based on alleged negligence of the defendant. The Admiralty judge had set the writ aside on the grounds that the subject-matter of the writ was not a dispute arising from an agreement between the plaintiff and the defendant. The Court of Appeal, sitting to hear the plaintiff's subsequent appeal, reversed the Admiralty judge's ruling on the

8. *The Eschersheim* [1976] 2 Lloyd's Rep. 1.
9. *The Antonis P. Lemos* [1984] 1 Lloyd's Rep. 464 (C.A.).

grounds that there were no such limiting words on the text of subpara. (h), that the 1952 Convention itself never implied any such restrictive interpretation and that provided that the claim in question arose out of an agreement of the nature specified it did not necessarily have to be an agreement between the plaintiff and the defendant.

It is an interesting and highly topical additional provision that subsection 2(e) – damage done by a ship – extends to claims in respect of a liability for oil pollution incurred under the United Kingdom's Merchant Shipping (Oil Pollution) Act 1971, (the United Kingdom's enactment of the Civil Liability Convention on Oil Pollution 1969) and also claims falling under the "Fund" Convention as enacted by the United Kingdom's Merchant Shipping Act 1974.

Time barring of statutory rights "in rem"

Statutory rights *in rem*, in exactly the same way as maritime liens, are subject to extinction by statutory time barring, the length of time allowed within which to bring action being determined by the nature of the claim. For example, in the case of cargo loss or damage (a claim conferring *in rem* rights but not a maritime lien), the period is *one* year from the date the goods were or should have been discharged. This is assuming that the contract of carriage was subject to the Hague Rules or the Hague/Visby Rules, the latter being incorporated mandatorily into English law through the United Kingdom Carriage of Goods by Sea Act 1971, which took effect in June 1977.

As to maritime claims which fall within the list detailed in section 20(2) of the Supreme Court Act 1981 and which have not been specifically mentioned above as covered by a specific time limitation period or which are not caught by some particular statutory or other special legal limitation period, the laches doctrine will continue to apply in respect of actions brought *in rem*. But, the action *in rem*, and this cannot be repeated too often, cannot be brought (i.e. a writ issued) *after* the ship has changed ownership.

A writ "in rem" and a warrant of arrest contrasted

It is in the writer's opinion misleading if not legally incorrect to describe statutory rights *in rem* as "statutory liens". First, it gives the impression that they are rights in the nature of a lien which does not strictly conform to what must be the true essence of a statutory right *in rem*, namely that it is a device used against a ship to found jurisdiction and with a view also to obtaining security in some form. It should be emphasized that *arrest itself* is not these days necessary to found jurisdiction. It is sufficient to institute *in rem* action only. In practical terms, this means the issuing and serving on the named property of a writ *in rem*. The arrest process, as distinct from mere *in rem* proceedings, gives the added advantage to the arrestor/claimant that he may thereby obtain from the owner of the arrested property adequate alternative prejudgment security. The fine distinction between the service of a writ *in rem* on the defendant property and the service of a warrant of arrest may, however, be of academic interest only.

In strict legal procedure, and since 1883, a writ *in rem* and a warrant of arrest are separate documents but in practice in the vast majority of cases they are served at the same time on the *res*. If the cause of action is not time barred and if a writ has been allowed to lapse then in most cases a further writ can be issued. The criterion probably is have all reasonable (*not all possible*) steps been taken to serve the writ? If a writ has expired, a fresh writ can be issued provided that the ship named in the expired writ has not been transferred into new (beneficial) ownership since the original writ was issued.

Under Order 6, rule 8 of the Rules of the Supreme Court one can apply for an extension of the validity of the writ. *The Helene Roth*[10] is authority for the rule that solicitors who issue a writ have a duty to serve it promptly. Renewal is not to be granted as a matter of course.

When do liens and statutory rights "in rem" respectively come into being?

Liens tend, though not exclusively, to be the creatures of the common law and are rights which spring into being and accrue at the time of the original cause of action. This cannot be said of a statutory right *in rem*. Judicial interpretation of this statutory authority, for example *The Monica S*[11] makes it clear that the right does not pre-exist the taking of the action and that until action is taken, for example by the concrete act of issuing a writ naming the *res*, the right does not come into being. This is a fundamental and legally inescapable difference

---

10. *Supra*, fn. 1.
11. *The Monica S* [1967] 2 Lloyd's Rep. 113.

between the right *in rem* as granted by old-established statutory authority and the common-law inspired lien.

Actions "in rem" distinguished from actions "in personam"

One of the most important things to realize if a full understanding is to be had of the action *in rem* under English legal thinking is that it is an action *entirely independent* of an action *in personam*. It is not something which is ancillary to it. It is against the *ship*, not its owner, and judgment may eventually be given against the ship and thus the whole process may be "pushed through" that far without even the owners of the *res* having appeared to answer the writ. Why should they? The writ was served on the ship, not them. Their personal liability is, under English legal thinking, not "under the spotlight", it is irrelevant. An action *in rem* can culminate (though in practice seldom does) in a judgment *in rem* which is "good as against all the world". A shipowner *may* take part in an action *in rem* if he thinks it appropriate to defend his property. But it is essentially an action against his property (*in rem*) not against him.

It is nevertheless not possible in an Admiralty action *in rem* for a summary judgment to be given without the claim which lies behind the action having been first verified by affidavit evidence and in any event the probability is also that the defendant to the action would seek to show that there were issues deserving of being tried so that leave to defend either conditionally or unconditionally should be granted rather than summary judgment be given. Once having entered an appearance to an Admiralty action *in rem*, the defendant has thereby submitted himself *personally* to the jurisdiction of the Admiralty Court and from that point on the action proceeds against him as an action *in personam* concurrent with the action *in rem*.

The action *in rem* is therefore substantively different from an action *in personam*. The restrictions applicable to the latter are not so applicable to the former.

Do not confuse the difference between a seizure effected collateral to an action *in personam* against a ship's owners and an action *in rem per se*. The former does not subsequently bar the latter.

In rem is essentially an *alternative* action and not one which is an adjunct to or springing from a personal action. Why does it enjoy such popularity among maritime claimants world-wide? Because it is immensely convenient and has practical advantages over a personal action. For example, it may be difficult to get court approval to serve a personal writ of summons outside the jurisdiction of the court which issues the writ.

By issuing a writ *in rem* and then waiting until one can pounce on the *res* when it comes within the court's territorial jurisdiction one has an excellent means of "persuasion" to get the owner of the *res* within one's grasp. Serving of the writ founds jurisdiction and enables the obtaining of adequate security in lieu in addition to the satisfaction of knowing that if one does eventually obtain a judgment against the owner of the *res*, one will, within and subject to the terms of the security, get ultimate satisfaction. It should be noted, however, that the writ *in rem* cannot be served *outside* the jurisdiction.

What is beneficial ownership?

Beneficial ownership itself needs explanation because nowhere in any United Kingdom statute is it defined. The expression derives from the English law concept of *trust* ownership, of ships, for example, being owned and operated under the "cloak" of a trust – a nominee company holding property (a ship) in trust for a beneficiary (its parent). To determine who truly is beneficial owner of a vessel it must be investigated not only who is the legal owner of these shares but also who has an equitable interest and only thus by taking account of both legal *and* equitable ownership can beneficial ownership be determined. "Piercing the corporate veil" of registered ownership may be necessary in pursuit of such an investigation because English law does not require more than one owner to register himself, however many may own shares in the same vessel. It is questionable whether, in practical terms, the corporate veil can be pierced in the absence of evidence of fraud, for example, an apparent sale after the cause of action arose.

The necessity to determine beneficial ownership in order to satisfy the requirements of English law (as opposed to international Convention) and to ensure that there has been no improper or wrongful arrest can cause problems in English jurisdiction which do not arise in jurisdictions of those countries which have no concept of trust ownership. It is here, basically, that English law has always been "out of step with" international trends. The Arrest Convention refers throughout to "owning", "ownership", "owned by", – a simpler concept than the more complex English notion, avoiding the need in some cases to "pierce" the "corporate veil" of corporate ownership (as English judges have described it) – to determine true, real, underlying or beneficial ownership. Because of the requirement of English statutory (Admiralty) law to determine *beneficial* ownership, the courts have invested themselves with the discretionary power to investigate beneficial ownership, to "pierce the corporate veil" or facade of nominee or registered ownership and look behind (see *dicta* in *The Aventicum*[12]). Subsequently in *The Maritime Trader*[13] the Admiralty judge stated his view that a court should only use that power if there was a genuine likelihood that the owning company (legally registered as such) was formed merely as a device to hide the ship away from being used as security or sold to satisfy a judgment. *But*, can the necessary evidence be adduced other than through the process of court-ordered discovery? And how or where can such an order be secured at the early stage before the writ *in rem* has been issued?

The right to arrest an alternative ship

Britain's enactment of the Arrest Convention introduced statutorily the idea that the right to arrest an alternative vessel, as opposed to the offending or involved vessel, rested on the determination as to whether that ship selected as alternative was owned as respects all its shares by the person who would be liable on the claim. The actual wording of the provision (known as the "sister ship" provision in the statute) may be found originally stated in section 3(4) of the 1956 Act (now replaced by section 21(4) of the Supreme Court Act 1981). Prior to the bringing into effect of the 1981 Act, English courts had placed a restrictive interpretation on the right to seek out and arrest an alternative vessel, so restrictive that the provision allowing for such alternative arrest in the 1956 statute (section 3(4)) was known as the "sister ship" provision. This was because the courts had required there to be a *common ownership link* between the offending or involved vessel and the alternative ship selected for arrest (see *dicta* in *The*

---

12. *The Aventicum* [1978] 1 Lloyd's Rep. 184.
13. *The Maritime Trader* [1981] 2 Lloyd's Rep. 153.

Eschersheim[14]). The two vessels had to be under the *same beneficial ownership* as respects all their shares.

This restrictive interpretation placed a bar on arrest procedure in the following hypothetical but in reality very likely happening. Shipowner A time charters his ship X to B. B commits a breach of charter. A wishes to arrest ship Y wholly beneficially owned by B. He cannot, under the judicial interpretation of the 1956 Act (section 3(4)), because there is no common property ownership between ship X and ship Y.

Just prior to the bringing into effect of the Supreme Court Act 1981 a significant law suit received a hearing in the English Admiralty Court, subsequently being taken to appeal – *The Span Terza*.[15] The dispute almost pre-empted the about-to-be-introduced statute. The facts (very similar to the hypothetical example given earlier) were:

the plaintiffs owned ship X which they had time-chartered to the defendants. The defendants owned ship Y (the *Span Terza*). They were allegedly liable for unpaid hire and damages to the plaintiffs in respect of ship X charter. The plaintiffs sought, pursuant to *in rem* rights under the 1956 Act, to arrest ship Y (the *Span Terza*) under the "sister ship" provision (section 3(4)). What was the real issue to be determined was whether section 3(4) could be successfully used to arrest a vessel under the ownership (beneficial) of someone *not* the beneficial owner of the offending, or more correctly on these facts, the involved vessel.

The case had the unique experience of being "rushed" from the court of first instance to the Court of Appeal on the same day because of the urgency, so far as the plaintiff arrestor was concerned, of the need to know. The Court of Appeal, by a majority only, decided that there did *not* have to be an ownership link between the involved ship and that selected alternatively for arrest.

Strangely enough, one of the very few precedents which the Appeal judges had to go on and which conformed with their eventual decision was a decision of the Singapore Court of Appeal (*The Permina 108*[16]) where on similar facts the court had concluded that there was no reason why the offending and alternative ships should be under common ownership for the arrest action to succeed.

So at last after 30 years of restrictive interpretation of the section 3(4) statutory provision, the courts adopted the liberal interpretation.

14. *Supra*, fn. 8.
15. *The Span Terza* [1982] 1 Lloyd's Rep. 225.
16. [1978] 1 Lloyd's Rep. 311.

But as at 1st January 1982 the new statute took effect and seems to have "liberalized" the procedure, statutorily in any event.

Perhaps it is the word "charterer" and the meaning of it as used in the statute that has caused much of the conflict in judicial views. The 1952 Arrest Convention quite clearly in its Article 3, para. 4, allows the arrest of a ship *owned* by a demise charterer who is potentially liable on the claim. English statute law, developed as a result of the 1952 Convention, failed to draw such a clear-cut distinction between a charterer by demise and any other variety of charterer and, as a result, the restrictive interpretation became the vogue and the requirement of common ownership between the offending and the alternative "arrestable" ship also became the vogue to the extent that the expression "sister ship" arrest became common talk, misleading though that expression now is in the 1980s as a result of the introduction of the 1981 (replacement) statute following closely upon it. None of this judicial conflict would have arisen if England's legislation drafters had, in designing the *1956* statute, included in their draft Article 3(4) of the *Convention* reading as follows:

> When in the case of a charter by demise of a ship the charterer and not the registered owner is liable in respect of a maritime claim relating to that ship, the claimant may arrest such ship or any other ship in the ownership of the charterer by demise, subject to the provisions of this Convention, but no other ship in the ownership of the registered owner shall be liable to arrest in respect of such maritime claims.

The following words also appear at the conclusion of the above paragraph:

> The provisions of this paragraph shall apply to any case in which a person other than the registered owner of a ship is liable in respect of a maritime claim relating to that ship.

These concluding words quite clearly and categorically indicate that there need not be an ownership link between the involved ship and the alternative ship. The English statute, however, either deliberately or inadvertently, did not implement that particular paragraph of the Convention and thus English law "went off at a tangent" and was diverted easily into the restrictive judicial interpretation as to what alternative ship could be arrested.

Let us now look at the equivalent provision in the 1981 statute. Section 21(4) reads:

In the case of any such claim as is mentioned in section 20(2)(e) to (r), where
    (a) the claim arises in connection with a ship; and
    (b) the person who would be liable on the claim in an in personam ("the relevant person") was, when the cause of action arose, the owner or charterer of, or in possession or in control of, the ship,
an action in rem may (whether or not the claim gives rise to a maritime lien on that ship) be brought in the High Court against
    (1) that ship, if at the time when the action is brought the relevant person is either the beneficial owner of that ship as respects all its shares or the charterer of it under a charter by demise; or
    (2) any other ship of which, at the time when the action is brought, the relevant person is the beneficial owner as respects all the shares in it.

Although the section as it is literally worded still leaves a slight possibility that the court *could* apply the "restrictive" interpretation, it would be a very narrow-minded judge of a conservative frame of mind who dared to do so now that demise charterers are categorized in their own right and that the word "charterer" itself is thus the more naturally open to being defined as any type of charterer. It should not be thought that the words in brackets ". . . whether or not the claim gives rise to a maritime lien on that ship . . ." changes the character of a maritime lien at all. They do not. All these words mean is that a claimant who happens to have a lien against a particular ship *may*, if *that* vessel is unavailable, take *in rem* action against an alternative ship.

Is it possible to arrest the same ship twice?

The tempting answer is *no*. But it is not quite so simple as that. The point came to be considered before the English Admiralty Court in 1982 (*The Despina G.K.*[17]). This ship *was* seized (arrested) twice. First in a Swedish port in 1976 by cargo insurers. They had obtained an arrest order from the Stockholm Admiralty Court, the subject-matter of their claim being cargo loss/damage on a voyage from Antwerp to Mogadishu. The Swedish court considered itself competent to hear and determine the case and not only condemned the ship's owners to pay an amount in settlement, plus interest and costs but also, strange to English legal ears, awarded the claimants a maritime lien on the vessel for their claim. (Such liens in England are not awarded by the

17. *The Despina G.K.* [1982] 2 Lloyd's Rep. 555.

courts but spring from the general maritime law and in any event are not acquired in respect of this type of claim.) The Swedish Court of Appeal condoned this ruling, qualifying it only in that the judgment could be enforced only on the vessel and not on any other asset of the owner.

The Greek shipowner satisfied most of the judgment, leaving only a small balance outstanding and before any change in ownership of the vessel the not-fully-satisfied claimants issued a writ in the *English* Admiralty Court and caused a warrant of arrest to be served on the ship when she entered an English port.

Perhaps it was a good thing that this dispute did, as fate would have it, come before the English court because the judge did have the opportunity to give his views ("for the benefit of practitioners", as he put it) in the light of the very recently introduced 1981 Supreme Court Act. He emphasized that the rules of Admiralty law relating to the arising and enforcing of maritime liens, on the one hand, must be distinguished from the *statutory* right *in rem*/arrest, on the other hand. There was, of course, a vital difference between a lien, which was a right against the vessel as the instrumentality of wrongdoing and which survived against it through changes of ownership until the rendering of a judgment in court, and a statutory right of arrest which depended for its very existence on the issuing of a writ *before* any change of ownership. But in addition English law also required a fine distinction to be made between (i) the bringing of an action *in rem* against a ship for whatever reason, and (ii) the executing of a judgment obtained as a result of such action.

Because of this latter distinction the judge decided that a judgment creditor who has obtained a final judgment against a shipowner pursuant to proceedings *in rem* in a foreign (in this instance Swedish) Admiralty Court is permitted to bring a subsequent action in England if necessary to complete the execution of the judgment *provided that* the vessel is still in the same ownership of the judgment debtor at the time of the re-arrest. This was not to admit, so emphasized the Admiralty judge, that the beneficiary of a foreign court judgment enjoyed a status similar to the holder of a maritime lien under English law.

What, to the writer, this piece of case-law illustrates is that an action *of an in rem nature* may *still* be pursued against a vessel if a *previous* arrest of the *same* ship has been founded upon a right *in rem* which has eventually become a judgment *in rem* but which has remained not fully satisfied. In other words, if a previous arrest could correctly be defined as a maritime attachment either under the law of the country where that earlier arrest took place or under English law, then an English Admiralty Court will permit the second arrest as being merely to enforce the foreign judgment. What can*not* happen under any circumstances is for the same vessel to be arrested twice, *both* times being the putting into effect of an *in rem* right against the vessel whether or not the arrest is in enforcement of a maritime lien on the vessel.

What happens when there is a pre-existing contractual forum (or more convenient forum) different from the forum where arrest takes place?

It is a feature of English legal theory that the jurisdiction conferred on an Admiralty Court to issue writs *in rem* or warrants of arrest exists *independently* of any jurisdiction established by contractual agreement between the parties to a contract or alternatively to there existing a more proper convenient "forum" elsewhere in the world, taking account of the facts and circumstances surrounding the incident which gave rise to the claim. Thus the arresting court in practical terms may be neither of these things. Nevertheless, there is no pre-existing requirement of the jurisdiction to arrest that the arresting court should be properly the court contractually picked to examine the merits or the "right place" to consider a claim in tort. Once jurisdiction has been founded by proceedings *in rem* it is in the judge's discretion to decide whether he and his court should go on to examine the merits or to stay and/or transfer the proceedings to another (foreign) forum.

Lord Denning, M.R., in *The Fehmarn*[18] said: "I do not regard the choice of law in the contract as decisive; I prefer to look to see with what country the dispute is most closely concerned". Very compelling arguments would have to be put before the court if a successful attempt was to be made to retain jurisdiction in the face of an exclusive jurisdiction clause (i.e. one agreeing to the use of some foreign forum) in e.g. a contract of carriage contained in a bill of lading. In *The El Amria*[19] it was said that the parties cannot oust the

18. *The Fehmarn* [1957] 2 Lloyd's Rep. 551.
19. *The El Amria* [1980] 1 Lloyd's Rep. 390.

jurisdiction of the (arresting) court by agreement. The plaintiff must show strong reason why the courts should not give effect to an existing agreement to refer to a foreign jurisdiction.

If an English court whose aid has been invoked or, (in the language of the now-in-force Supreme Court Act 1981) before whom an action *in rem* has been brought, is informed that the plaintiff (arrestor) and the defendant (whose property has been served with the writ and who has probably given security in lieu) had voluntarily agreed with each other in, for example, their contract of carriage, that any disputes arising would be referred to a selected foreign forum, the matter is at the English judge's discretion as to whether he grants the defendant's application to stay proceedings in favour of that foreign court or whether he considers that the interests of achieving a just solution for both parties would be better served by retaining jurisdiction in defiance of the contractual arrangement. The best summary of the way the courts think on this point is probably to be found in Brandon, J.'s decision in *The El Amria*:[20]

Where plaintiffs sue in England in breach of an agreement to refer disputes to a foreign Court, and the defendant applies for a stay, the English Court, assuming the claim to be otherwise within its jurisdiction, is not bound to grant a stay but has a discretion whether to do so or not. The discretion should be exercised by granting a stay unless strong cause for not doing so is shown.

This was supported by (to take a random example) Sheen, J. in *The Atlantic Song*.[21] Lord Denning, while Master of the Rolls (senior judge in the Court of Appeal), let it be known that he preferred to look at the facts, circumstances and evidence thereon put before him and to see with which jurisdiction the issue(s) is/are *most closely connected*.

Clearly, such factors as the location and availability of witnesses and/or documentary evidence, the overall estimate of costs expected if the case was transferred to that contractually selected forum as compared with those if it was retained, and – a very important factor – the question of whether if it *was* transferred the plaintiff's interests would be seriously and unfairly prejudiced, for example because he might find himself time-barred and thus left wholly without a remedy.

The party (plaintiff) opposing the application to stay must therefore show, in legal phrase, "*strong cause*" why the proceedings should not be stayed if he is to defeat the natural inclination of an

20. *Supra*, fn. 19.
21. *The Atlantic Song* [1983] 2 Lloyd's Rep. 394.

English judge to respect and uphold the foreign jurisdiction clause which, after all, contains the original voluntary mutual wishes of the disputants.

One of the cardinal principles of Admiralty Court jurisprudence is that mere balance of convenience is *not* sufficient ground for depriving a plaintiff of the advantages of an action properly brought in the arresting court. In this respect English judges still draw inspiration from the case of *MacShannon* v. *Rockware Glass Ltd.*[22] On the vast majority of occasions there is no *natural* forum resulting from the consensus of facts and circumstances surrounding the incident. In *The Traugutt*[23] the bill of lading law was Belgian *if* cargo was shipped from a Belgian port, otherwise it was to be Polish law. The ship was Polish, her officers were Polish, the owners' principal place of business was in Poland. An action *in rem* had been brought *in England* against a sister ship in respect of alleged loss/damage to cargo shipped from Antwerp to Bombay. The defendant shipowners sought to stay the English action on the grounds that England was not a convenient forum (*forum non conveniens*, to use the formal language), that in any event a dispute to be resolved in accordance with Belgian law should appropriately be brought before a Belgian court. There was admittedly, so the court was told, a difference between Belgian and English legal attitudes towards the question of a corporate shipowner's *personal* fault depriving him of his limitation rights but that fell short of saying that justice could substantially be done at less inconvenience and expense than in England. English was the language of the contractual documents, England was the place of residence of relevant expert witnesses. The "balance of convenience" favoured English jurisdiction.

Staying proceedings in favour of arbitration

Bearing well in mind that the purpose of maritime arrest procedure is twofold, namely (i) to obtain security for a maritime claim, and (ii) to secure the defendant's appearance and/or to found jurisdiction over the *in personam* defendant, one question not yet fully resolved is how far may arrest action be pursued for the sole purpose of obtaining security in respect of a future *arbitration* award. This requires a basic

22. *MacShannon* v. *Rockware Glass Ltd.* [1978] A.C. 795.
23. *The Traugutt* (1984) LMLN 113.

understanding of how arbitration differs in principle from legal action through the courts. Arbitration could be described as litigation in the "private sector" as distinguished from resort to the courts which could be described as litigation in the "public sector" (the distinction bears comparison with public and private sector medicine under the United Kingdom system of social security). But arbitration is essentially a *personal* matter, arising from contract (the arbitration entered into voluntarily and on their own mutually agreed terms by both parties). It follows from this basic thinking that *in rem* action, allowed under statutory powers and on the basis of court jurisdiction to hear and determine a dispute, should not by definition be used pursuant to a matter which the parties themselves have already agreed to take before a *private* (arbitration) tribunal. But, the United Kingdom is a party to the Convention on the Mutual Enforcement of Arbitration Awards (1958) and has enacted its provisions in the Arbitration Act 1975. One of the provisions of the Act is to make it mandatory upon an arresting court to stay proceedings in favour of arbitration where there is in existence an arbitration agreement (international as opposed to domestic, international meaning that the parties to the agreement reside in different sovereign territories). The court's powers in this regard are not discretionary, it is emphasized, but mandatory, i.e. the wording is not "*may* stay" but "*shall* stay" (section 1).

What happens to security obtained as a result of arrest action?

So, supposing a ship is arrested to obtain security where an arbitration agreement pre-exists, the arrest action and security is given in exchange for a court order releasing the vessel. What should the court do about the security if it is obliged to stay the proceedings? It should also be emphasized that the court's duty is to *stay not* to dismiss the proceedings, i.e. to stop the proceedings for the time being. Should the presiding judge discharge or release the security? Would that not be "unfair" on the plaintiff/arrestor? The judge has three alternatives:

(a) to release the security;
(b) to allow it to be retained;
(c) to call for alternative security in its place.

English statute law left a hiatus on the subject when attempting to enact the Arrest Convention of 1952, leaving the Admiralty judges of the day to "plug the gap" as best they could. During the 1960s and 1970s this was one man – Brandon, J. (now elevated to higher things) and there may have been a resultant over-purity in judicial thinking. (See *The Cap Bon*;[24] *The Golden Trader*;[25] and *The Rena K*[26].)

English law regards an arbitration, as we have seen, as purely personal, giving rise to a right to proceed *in personam* only, but does not prohibit the taking of Admiralty action *in rem* against a ship when an arbitration agreement has pre-existed a dispute arising. In fact, a right *in rem* survives even the award itself and subject to the ship not having changed ownership in the interim can be harnessed to enforce the award. Brandon, J., however, in *The Cap Bon*[27] case, stressed that security obtained as a result of proceedings *in rem* against a ship could not be used to satisfy an arbitration award (i.e. the fruits of a different and unrelated forum). This view, known as the "*Cap Bon* principle", has been judicially respected ever since.

Set against that judicial interpretation of the scope of security furnished through *in rem* action must be considered the judge's discretion – under powers granted at any rate by the Arbitration Act of 1950 – to ensure that before legal proceedings are stayed, satisfactory alternative arrangements are made in protection of the maritime claimant's interests. That could and most likely would include the furnishing of sufficient *alternative* security to cover the eventual arbitration award. Hence two judicial theories emerged, the right to retain security given so that it survived the staying of proceedings in favour of arbitration; and the right to order suitable alternative security on the basis that the original security necessarily "died" with the granting of a stay.

In *The Rena K*,[28] Brandon, J., considered that the court had a duty, if a stay was mandatory, to protect the plaintiff's interests and to decide what to do about security already given as a result of the Admiralty action. He did, however, stress that there should be an unconditional release of the security if the distinct probability was that the stay of proceedings in favour of arbitration would be final.

---

24. *The Cap Bon* [1967] 1 Lloyd's Rep. 543.
25. *The Golden Trader* [1974] 1 Lloyd's Rep. 378.
26. *The Rena K*. [1978] 1 Lloyd's Rep. 545.
27. See fn. 24, *supra*.
28. See fn. 26, *supra*.

This was in accordance with the principle that security given pursuant to an Admiralty Court (*in rem*) action need only be honoured in the event either of an eventual court judgment or an amicable settlement, *not* an arbitration award.

Value can be drawn from a study of what the Admiralty judge in *The Vasso* (formerly *Andria*) case said.[29] The plaintiff's motive was said to be immaterial in determining whether the court was rightly exercising its powers of arrest. But what it should *not* do is to use its powers to provide security, for a possible award in a *pending* arbitration. In *The Vasso* the vessel's P. & I. Club had furnished their undertaking to get the ship released after her arrest at the suit of the cargo owner. The writ *in rem* had been served out of fear that the ship was about to be sold and that any assets out of which an eventual award might be satisfied might rapidly disappear into "thin air". Robert Goff, L.J. (on appeal) reaffirmed that as English law presently stands the purpose of the power to arrest a ship in an action *in rem* is to provide security *for that action* and *not* in other proceedings such as arbitration. But his judicial pronouncement, he admitted, might be of short-lived significance in the face of the imminent coming into effect of section 26 of the Civil Jurisdiction and Judgments Act 1982.[30] As it happened *The Vasso* court had a special reason for releasing the Club's undertaking – the failure of the arresting party to disclose in his affidavit that proceedings arising from an *ad hoc* arbitration agreement were in progress. That alone was an abuse of the Admiralty Court process.

At the time of preparation of this section, the latest case on this particular issue to come before the Admiralty Court (March 1984) and very rapidly before the Appeal Court (April 1984) was *The Tuyuti*.[31] The ship had carried wool cargoes under bills of lading containing a London arbitration clause and also opting for English law. It had also carried screws under bills containing an exclusive Uruguayan jurisdiction clause – the country of the carrier's business residence.

Writs were issued by the cargo owners generally but they had failed to identify in the endorsement to the writ (as required by the Rules of the Supreme Court, Order 6, rule 2) who owned which individual cargo, leaving the defendant shipowner somewhat under-informed.

29. *The Vasso*, formerly *Andria* [1984] 1 Lloyd's Rep. 235.
30. This section came into force on 20th September 1984.
31. *The Tuyuti* [1984] 2 Lloyd's Rep. 51.

Concurrent with the writ the cargo owner plaintiffs had obtained an arrest warrant but had not served it due to lack of suitable opportunity. Service of the *writ*, however, had been acknowledged voluntarily which had the effect of turning the proceedings into *in personam*. Subsequently, the plaintiffs and the defendant entered into an arbitration agreement covering all cargoes which potentially brought all the disputes within the relevance and scope of the Arbitration Act 1975, section 1. The plaintiffs acknowledged that the court had a mandatory duty to stay re the wool cargoes but not re the other (screws) cargo in connection with which there was only an *ad hoc* arbitration agreement arranged *subsequent* to the *in rem* proceedings. The cargo owners' main, and understandable, fear was that the carrying vessel owner was probably financially incapable of satisfying any eventual arbitration award. *But*, this does not fall within the accepted interpretation of an "arbitration agreement being inoperative or incapable of performance" which was the sole available reason for avoiding the statutory duty to stay court proceedings under section 1 of the 1975 Act. Admiralty judge Sheen stayed both the legal proceedings (converted into *in personam* by the defendant owner's voluntary acceptance of service) *and* execution of the warrant of arrest.

The Appeal Court reversed the latter decision saying that a distinction must be made between the proceedings and the warrant of arrest. It held that proceedings must be stayed if they contravened an arbitration agreement but that did not include the execution of a warrant which might in the future be needed to provide security for a revived action *in rem*. The warrant was therefore *not* set aside.

Relevance of section 26 of the Civil Jurisdiction and Judgments Act 1982

This section became effective on 20th September 1984 and has removed the need for further judicial searching on the point. The *Cap Bon* principle is dead. Where Admiralty proceedings are stayed (or dismissed) in favour not only of arbitration but of an overseas forum, for instance, the court may order the retention of security furnished or the provision of alternative security to obtain an eventual arbitration award. Section 26 will ensure that a plaintiff is secured against *all* eventualities. If the arbitral process "misfires" or is incapable of performance he can use the security by going back to the Admiralty Court to complete his Admiralty action since the action was only stayed, *not* dismissed. If the arbitral process succeeds the security originally obtained can be used legally to enforce that award.

Can "in rem" action be taken against more than one ship?

In *The Banco* case[32] it was decided that Admiralty jurisdiction can only be invoked against *one* vessel of the defendant. Invocation in this sense means *service* of the writ. There is nothing to prevent the issuing of a writ against *all* of the defendant's ships but service on *one only* is permitted. The cases of *The Banco* and *The Monica S*[33] have become confused. What is the true test for determining when a plaintiff has become a secured creditor? Is it, as Brandon, J., said in *The Monica S*, when he invokes the jurisdiction of the Admiralty Court by *issuing* a writ or is it not until he *serves* it and takes arrest action, as the court in *The Banco appeared* to say?

When has "in rem" action been effectively taken?

In *Re Aro Co. Ltd.*[34] Oliver, J., *at first instance*, followed *The Banco* reasoning – the plaintiff is not a secured creditor until he *serves* his writ. But in reversing that decision the Court of Appeal recommended getting rid of the test as to whether the court's jurisdiction had or had not been invoked and instead concentrating the mind on whether they had or had not a right as against all the world which they could enforce against the vessel as their object of security. Answer: *yes*, they could *if* they had *issued* the writ. It could thereafter be served on the ship despite title to the ship having passed from the liquidator (in that particular case) on to a bona fide transferee for value.

However, arguments regarding invocation are, since the 1981 Act took effect, academic only because the criterion for invocation has been replaced by different wording.

At this point a few comments are in order on the relationship of an action *in rem*/arrest to a proceeding for liquidation of a company or a bankruptcy. Most ships nowadays are owned by corporate entities so

32. *The Banco* [1971] 1 Lloyd's Rep. 49.
33. See fn. 11 *supra*.
34. *Re Aro Co. Ltd.* [1980] 2 W.L.R. 453.

a writ *in rem* has been issued, though not necessarily served, prior to the commencement of the winding up proceedings there is judicial authority to support the view that a claimant should be allowed nevertheless to proceed *in rem* and stand in the same secured position as if he had possessed a maritime lien. (*Re Aro Co. Ltd., infra.*)

The holder of a statutory right *in rem*, however, who has not issued a writ prior to the commencement of the winding up proceedings shall not, generally speaking, be allowed to proceed, since to do so would elevate him to the position of a secured creditor by allowing him to make perfect what prior to the winding up proceedings was imperfect by reason of his having failed even to issue a writ.

As an illustration of the practical operation of these legal rules, the facts of *Re Aro Co. Ltd.*[36] do serve admirably.

The vessel *Aro* was owned by Aro Co. Ltd., a one-ship company. A claim dating back to 1974 for short delivery of cargo was still unsatisfied. The claimant was Texaco. In March 1977 the Shell Company had a claim for their unpaid bill for bunkers supplied. Shell issued a writ *in rem* and in May of that year arrested the ship. Texaco in the July following, seeking to protect their interests, filed a *praecipe* in the Admiralty Registry under Order 75, rule 14 of the Rules of the Supreme Court. This caused the entry in the caveat book of a caveat against release of the arrested vessel. A day later Texaco issued a writ *in rem* and a writ *in personam* against the vessel's owners. Texaco could have served the writ, but did not. To do so was unnecessary because of the protection they had already acquired for themselves by observing the caveat procedure (some call this the "early warning system").[37]

In November 1977 a petition for the winding up of the owning company was presented and a winding up order made in January 1978. Shell had actually effected arrest and were therefore acknowledged as secured creditors. Eventually, in October 1978, the ship was sold by the Admiralty Marshal. It was up to the court to decide how Texaco stood. Their writ, though unserved, had been renewed although their writ *in personam* had expired. They had also renewed their caveat which had a life of six months only, unless renewed.

The court of first instance (a Companies Court) dismissed

---

36. See fn. 34, *supra.*

37. It is the intention of the English courts not to disturb or discourage the very sensible practice (briefly described on page 49) that second or subsequent claimants against a vessel can protect their position more conveniently and certainly at less cost by entering caveats against release rather than by effecting arrest after arrest on the second vessel.

ENGLAND AND WALES   29

that we are substantially concerned with liquidation proceedings and
not personal bankruptcy. What a maritime claimant will like to know
is whether matters of shipowner insolvency come within the juridical
sphere of the Admiralty Court or whether they are properly the
province of a non-Admiralty Court, and furthermore how and when
can he secure his interests against a company in compulsory or
voluntary liquidation.

The Companies Act 1948 provides that "when any company
registered in England is being wound up by the court, any attachment, sequestration, distress or execution put in force against the
estate or effects of the company after the commencement of the
winding up will be void to all intents". (Section 228(1).)

The phrase "time of commencement of a winding up" is inter-
preted in section 229 as defined in respect of a *voluntary* winding up as
the time of the company's resolution to voluntarily wind up so that a
petition for winding up *after* such resolution shall be caught by section
228. In the case of any other winding up the commencement shall be
considered to be the presentation of the petition to wind up.

What is meant by "sequestration"? To all intents and purposes, an
arrest. Sequestration (arrest) and attachment are different as briefl
indicated on page 14. In *The Constellation*[35] arrest and sale i
Admiralty are equivalent to sequestration and execution in th
language of the Companies Act.

Other provisions of the Companies Act 1948 (sections 226 and 23
temper the strict "final" effect of section 228 by allowing a cou
discretion to permit an action *in rem* to subsist against the property
the company under liquidation. Thus, an arrest prior to commenc
ment of a winding up (whether compulsory or voluntary) *may*, at
court's discretion, go through without hindrance whether that arr
is pursuant to a maritime lien or a mere statutory right to procee
rem. If the holder of a *maritime lien* has failed to enforce his lien prio
the commencement of a winding up, he need not worry unduly si
the court will be likely to exercise its discretion in his favour even a
a winding up order has come into existence. This is a perfectly log
extension of the theory that a maritime lien holder is a sec
creditor even as far back as the original arising of the cause of ac
upon which his claim is founded.

As to whether such judicial favour would be exercised in the ca
a statutory right *in rem* holder is a little more doubtful but if, even

35. *The Constellation* [1965] 2 Lloyd's Rep. 538.

Texaco's application for leave under section 231 of the Companies Act 1948 to continue their *in rem* action against the vessel pending in the Admiralty Court, despite the fact that a winding up order had already been made. It based its decision on the fact that the writ (*in rem*) had not been served on the ship arrested and that thus the security for their claim was not perfected. To grant them leave would have given them precedence over other unsecured creditors and would have permitted them to "perfect an imperfection".

They appealed, and the Court of Appeal allowed their appeal. The appeal judges viewed the issue of the writ (by Texaco) as bestowing on Texaco the right to serve it. That it had not been served was irrelevant. The appeal judges refused to base their decision solely on the service or not of the writ and to regard that as the sole test of whether a creditor had secured status or not. They insisted that judges should have unfettered discretion and that this was the legislative intention of section 231. A claimant who has *issued* a writ *in rem* prior to the commencement of a winding up should, in general, be allowed to continue his action. As here, a claimant who has issued a writ and entered a caveat against release if the ship has already been arrested by another party should be treated as if he had arrested her himself.

The appeal judges reaffirmed the object of suing *in rem* – to obtain security and to acquire the right to arrest and detain the ship (or the property which is the subject of the *in rem* suit). The issue of a writ *in rem* before transfer of the ship's ownership preserves the claimant's right to serve the writ after transfer (see *The Monica S, supra*, pages 13, 28). It was said in *The Monica S*: "it is the arrest which actually gives the claimant security, but a preliminary to arrest is the acquisition by the institution of a cause *in rem*, of the right to arrest".

Thus, said the Court of Appeal, the test should not be whether the jurisdiction of the Admiralty Court has been invoked (by service on the ship) but rather whether the claimant can say truthfully that before the presentation of the winding up petition (or the resolution to liquidate if it be voluntary) he has a right "against all the world" which he can assert and make effective. If he can, then the vessel is encumbered with that charge (albeit it is not a maritime lien). Thus, in the *Aro* case Texaco, as plaintiff, should be and was, as a result of the action they had taken, to all intents and purposes a secured creditor for the purposes of the exercise of the court's discretion under section 231 of the Companies Act 1948.

The overriding thought in the appeal judges' minds was that the exercise of their discretion should be unfettered so that what was fair and just in any given situation should be uppermost in the judges' minds.

Sovereign immunity

Doctrine of absolute immunity

More and more sovereigns these days are "stepping down from their thrones into the market place". Stated more prosaically, more ships, used for commercial purposes, are becoming owned (either wholly or substantially) and controlled by governments or departments of governments. To name a few countries which have State-owned or controlled fleets – Ghana, Malaysia, Kuwait, India and Mauritius. English law, prior to the Second World War, pursued a doctrine of absolute immunity. No matter what was the use to which a ship was being put, a sovereign-owner of it enjoyed immunity from the interference/process of the courts of a foreign sovereign State.

The Cristina case.[38] This doctrine was epitomized in a case which arose just prior to the Second World War and out of the Spanish Civil War which preceded it by a brief period. The English Admiralty Court declined to offer its aid to the private Spanish owners of a Spanish vessel, *Cristina*, which had been requisitioned by the de facto government (of Spain) when the latter placed a master of their own choice in charge of the ship during a call at a port in South Wales (i.e. within the jurisdiction of the High Court in London). English law in those days would not countenance a foreign sovereign being forced into an appearance in an English civil court.

Changing trends after the Second World War

The trend began to change after the Second World War. To put it more accurately international law began to have more and more influence on English law. English maritime law, in particular, began to follow international law principles because the declared aim of the judiciary was to "keep in step with" international law. The case (*in rem*) which spelt the death throes of the long established but outdated

38. *The Cristina* [1938] A.C. 485.

doctrine of absolute immunity was *The Philippine Admiral*.[39] The facts concerned the construction of a ship by the Japanese as part of their overall commitment to effect reparations to the Philippine Government for war damages. The Philippine interests who acquired title contracted to sell it to X but retained title pending full payment of the purchase price. X operated her and in December 1972 chartered her to Y. All this while the Philippine Government remained the registered owner. While the ship was docked in Hong Kong *in rem* proceedings were taken out against her by Y (for breach of contract) and by Z (for unpaid disbursements). The Philippine Government (for strict accuracy the Philippine Reparations Commission), which was also defendant to the actions, applied to have the writs set aside on the grounds of their entitlement to sovereign immunity. They still had not been paid the full purchase price.

The issues finally came before the Judicial Committee of the Privy Council in London (the final appeal tribunal from the courts of certain Commonwealth countries) who ruled that the interest in the ship of the Philippine Government was more than illusory, despite the fact that at the time it was not actively operating the ship. Their interest was realistic. The ship was clearly intended for commercial use and not for public use and sovereign immunity should not be granted in respect of actions *in rem* under such circumstances. Although decisions of the Privy Council are not binding authority under the English law of precedent, they are extremely persuasive authority. The court carefully distinguished between actions *in personam* and actions *in rem* within the framework of sovereign immunity. Acts of a sovereign were to be divided into two categories:

  (a) *Acti de iure imperii* (acts of a government within the framework of government policy and with political motivation).
  (b) *Acti iure gestionis* (acts of a commercial nature).

So was ushered in the doctrine of *restricted immunity*.

Restricted immunity

The law said from this point on that there should be no distinction between the exposure of a ship to the process of a foreign court whether the ship was owned by a private individual (or corporate

39. *The Philippine Admiral* [1974] 2 Lloyd's Rep. 568.

personality) or by a government or the "wing" or "arm" of a government.

The drawing of a distinction between political acts and commercial acts is not a simple matter. People are divided in their opinions as to whether it is the *nature* of the act only which is the relevant point or whether it should be the *motivation* for the act. It seems generally accepted now that the nature of the act is the criterion and not the motivation. In *The I Congreso del Partido*[40] Lord Denning, M.R., expressed his own view: "when a government of a country enters into an ordinary trading transaction it cannot afterwards be permitted to repudiate it and get out of its liabilities by saying that it did it out of high government policy or foreign policy or any other policy". It could perhaps be said in this particular context that "once a commercial act, always a commercial act" and no amount of ingenious argument on motivation can transform it into a political act. A sovereign should not and cannot step *back up* on to his throne from the market place just as and when he feels like it.

The State Immunity Act 1978

The United Kingdom has crystallized the doctrine of restricted immunity by enshrining it in the State Immunity Act 1978. In its preamble this statute describes itself as being one to make new provision with respect to proceedings in the United Kingdom by or against other States; to provide for the effect of judgments in the courts of States parties to the European Convention on State Immunity; to make provision with respect to the immunities and privileges of Heads of States; and for connected purposes. It is intended to retain the broad principles of the old way of thinking, the absolute immunity of the sovereign in his personal capacity and of his property where use is restricted to public or purely sovereign use (section 1) but to establish exceptions from that, namely no immunity when, for example, vessels are used for commercial purposes.

For the purposes of this summary, section 10 is relevant. It is headed "Ships Used for Commercial Purposes". Subsection 2 of it reads:

40. *The I Congreso del Partido* [1980] 1 Lloyd's Rep. 23.

A state is not immune as respects – (a) an action in rem against a ship belonging to that State; or (b) an action in personam for enforcing a claim in connection with such a ship, if, at the time when the cause of action arose, the ship was in use or intended for use for commercial purposes.

This provision truly reflects the spirit of the Brussels Convention of 1926 on the subject of sovereign immunity of State-owned vessels. It underlines what should surely be a principle of natural justice that a government owner who uses his ship for trading purposes, for carrying cargoes for freight, or who lets his ship out for hire must recognize and accept the fact that he is liable to be sued on his commercial contracts and/or for wrongs or torts he commits, or his servants or agents commit, in the course of operating the vessel in the courts of any country which in the ordinary course may have jurisdiction to hear and determine the dispute which has arisen as a result.

Section 13(2)(*b*) of the State Immunity Act 1978 seems at first sight to be in direct conflict with section 10. It reads:

the property of a State shall not be subject to any process for the enforcement of a judgment or arbitration award or, in an action in rem, for its arrest, detention or sale.

However, subsection 4 of section 13 resolves this apparent contradiction by providing:

subsection (2)(*b*) above does not prevent the issue of any process in respect of property which is for the time being in use or intended for use for commercial purposes . . .

"Mareva" jurisdiction

The Mareva injunction analysed

All divisions of the High Court (including the Admiralty and Commercial Courts) possess what some describe, wrongly I believe, as an alternative jurisdiction to arrest or attachment, namely the *Mareva* injunction. I say wrongly because the principles and practice of an injunction of this nature differ in many important respects from the law of arrest as practised within the province of the Admiralty Court. The *Mareva* jurisdiction could be described in layman's language as keeping a watchful eye on "debt-dodgers".

The writer proposes to examine *Mareva* injunctions only in so far as it is necessary to compare them fully with actions *in rem* and the

process and effects of arrest and to distinguish their features,
advantages and disadvantages. What it is important to realize from
the outset is that an injunction of the *Mareva* type does *not*:

  (a) create in favour of the plaintiff any property right in the
  asset(s) which is/are the subject matter of the injunction.

It therefore does *not*:

  (b) put the plaintiff in any improved position or, if you like,
  "higher up the existing priority ladder" of other secured or
  even unsecured creditors.

It does *not*:

  (c) bar the way either to the defendant himself or to any third
  party, whose existing interest in the subject-matter may have
  been adversely affected, applying to the court to have the
  injunction lifted.

For example, the innocent charterer of a ship which is the
subject-matter of an injunction may convince a court that unless the
ship is freed from the "freezing" effect of the injunction so as to be able
to leave the jurisdiction to continue trading, his basic rights under the
charter's terms are being denied him (*The Rena K*[41]). Indeed, even the
shipowner himself can validly argue that he needs to sail his ship
away from the jurisdiction to reasonably carry on his business and
that his purpose in doing so is not solely to remove his ship from
exposure to being seized as security (*The Angel Bell*).[42]

In short, a *Mareva* injunction gives *in personam* rights *only*, i.e. rights
only against the defendant, whereas action *in rem* gives or creates,
when such action is taken, rights of property against the *res*. For
example, supposing a bank has been assigned the proceeds of an
arbitration award as security for a loan, the prior obtaining of a
Mareva injunction against that fund created by those proceeds, or so
much of it as was necessary to pay them off as creditor, did not work to
the plaintiff's advantage as the *Mareva* injunction would not "stand
up against" the bank's equitable assignment of the whole fund. The
injunction would therefore not be granted (*Pharoah's Plywood Co. Ltd.
v. Allied Wood Products Pte. Ltd.*).[43]

41. *The Rena K* [1979] Q.B. 377.
42. *Iraqi Ministry of Defence* v. *Arcepey Shipping Co. S.A.* (*The Angel Bell*) [1980] 1
Lloyd's Rep. 632.
43. (1980) LMLN 7.

By very definition, the interlocutory injunction is temporary by nature. This is emphasized by the fact that the freezing of assets may not bear any relationship to the cause of action upon which the injunction is founded. Thus, even if the applicant is successful in his action at trial as plaintiff, it does not automatically follow that the injunction is confirmed permanently.

The "bottom line" description of this type of injunction is that it is designed to prevent a potential defendant making himself "judgment-proof" by transferring his assets out of the jurisdiction where judgment may eventually be given against him or otherwise dealing with them (in the words of Lord Denning, M.R.).

In *Rasu Maritima S.A.* v. *Perusahaan Pertambangan Minyak Dan Gas Bumi (Pertamina)*[44] Lord Denning, M.R., was thought (mistakenly) to have equated a *Mareva* injunction to an *attachment*. He did not. He merely said that the *old* form of attachment and the *modern* form of interlocutory injunction achieved a broadly similar result. The two remedies cannot be wholly identified. An injunction is a purely personal matter whether it is against assets generally or particularized.

Origin of jurisdiction

Jurisdiction to grant this type of injunction originally sprang from section 45 of the Supreme Court of Judicature (Consolidation) Act 1925, but for some reason such injunctions did not really achieve widespread popularity, certainly in the world of shipping, until the mid-1970s. It was in fact the lawsuit of *Mareva Compania Naviera S.A.* v. *International Bulkcarriers S.A.*[45] which lent its name – *Mareva* – to this type of injunction. It is important to realize from the outset the well-defined limitations to a *Mareva* injunction. For a start, in order for such an injunction to be granted and imposed upon, for example, a defendant's bank account or even on a tangible asset – ship, cargo, freight, bunkers – there must be a genuine likelihood that the assets concerned will be dissipated, transferred or otherwise dealt with so as to make them unavailable to satisfy an eventual judgment and thus leave the plaintiff with an unenforceable judgment in his pocket.

44. *Rasu Maritima S.A.* v. *Perusahaan Pertambangan Minyak Dan Gas Bumi (Pertamina)* [1978] Q.B. 644.
45. *Mareva Compania Naviera S.A.* v. *International Bulkcarriers S.A.* [1975] 2 Lloyd's Rep. 509.

"Mareva" injunction clearly distinguished from lien or charge

What the *Mareva* injunction does *not* give to the plaintiff is any sort of lien or charge on the asset, nor any proprietary right. It is essentially a personal thing and not in the nature of a right *in rem*. For this very good reason it does not serve the same purpose as the process of arrest or attachment either by way of lien or by way of statutory *in rem* action. To take an example, if an attempt is made to "*Mareva*" a vessel and if the vessel is at the time under charter the charterer has only to show that his interests are prejudiced by the inability of the ship, albeit temporary, to leave the jurisdiction to achieve the lifting of the injunction.

Rights of third parties

Another interesting and recent example of the somewhat "touchy" business of the rights of *third*, innocent, parties being prejudiced by an injunction is *Clipper Maritime Co. Ltd. of Monrovia* v. *Mineralimportexport*.[46] The owners of a ship under charter obtained an injunction restraining the removal by the charterer of cargo and bunkers, both of which were the charterer's property, from the jurisdiction while the ship was calling at a port in South Wales. This put the port authority in a slight dilemma. Could they, in the routine exercise of their administrative powers, move the ship from its berth (not, of course, thereby from the jurisdiction of the court)? Not to do so would have easily meant loss of revenue from the non (productive) use of that berth. The continued presence of the ship at that berth might also have seriously hampered the general arrangements for other port users at that time. The Commercial Court ordered the shipowner/plaintiff to give a suitable undertaking to cover (i) the port authority's lost revenue, and (ii) any administrative out-of-pocket expenses, observing that any applications for *Mareva* injunctions are on an *ex parte* basis with innocent parties having no opportunity to be represented. Thus such innocent parties should be protected so far as is humanly possible.

The injunction thus does not enable the plaintiff to obtain as it were a "slice of the property" out of which he may eventually obtain satisfaction of his claim or of a judgment on his claim. It may have the effect of extracting suitable guarantees from the "*Marevaed*" defendant but this may be out of sheer desire not to be inconvenienced or

46. *Clipper Maritime Co. Ltd. of Monrovia* v. *Mineralimportexport* [1981] 1 W.L.R. 1262.

more likely out of a desire not to suffer the stigma or indignity in the eyes of his business customers or associates of being unable freely to handle his assets. In other words, security, if it is given in consideration of the lifting of the injunction, could at best be described as "quasi-security" only.

Mareva injunction not *right "in rem"*

Those who equate the *Mareva* injunction to an *in rem* right are making a basic error of definition. *Mareva* merely has the effect of preventing the defendant making himself "judgment-proof" without actually particularizing, identifying and seizing a specific asset to be used in a proprietary manner to pay off a judgment debt. It does not *of itself* found jurisdiction (like an Admiralty action *in rem*); it does not *of itself* represent a cause of action *ab initio*.

The Siskina Case[47] *(House of Lords Ruling)*

People talk of the "Siskina approach". *The Siskina* case took a very anatomical look at the *Mareva* injunction. The House of Lords refused to accept the argument that the *Mareva* injunction could and should be imposed by a commercial judge even if there was no potential cause of action linking the facts and circumstances with Britain and thus making an English court the proper forum (or, of course, possibly the contractual forum) for hearing and determining the disputed issue itself. In *The Siskina* the agreed (bill of lading) jurisdiction was Italian and the only "British connection" in the entire circumstances arising from the incident was that the insurance proceeds from the total loss (by sinking) of the *Siskina* were resting, at the time of the application for a *Mareva* injunction, in London and it was those (the only known assets of the defendant – the company was a "one-ship" company) which the plaintiff cargo owners wished to "freeze" and thus prevent being removed from the jurisdiction and dissipated beyond legal reach.

In *The Siskina* Lord Diplock said: "The purpose of this kind of interlocutory injunction against a foreign defendant is to ensure that there will be a fund available within the jurisdiction to meet any judgment obtained by the plaintiff in the High Court against a defendant who does not reside within the jurisdiction and has no place of business there".

47. *The Siskina* [1978] 1 Lloyd's Rep. 1.

The effect of section 25 of the Civil Jurisdiction and Judgments Act 1982

Section 25 of the Civil Jurisdiction and Judgments Act 1982 has caused a statutory reversal of the reasoning in *The Siskina* case. The 1982 Act is the implementation by the United Kingdom of the Convention of 1968 on Jurisdiction and the Enforcement of Judgments in Civil and Commercial Matters, together with the 1971 Protocol on interpretation of the 1968 Convention by the European Court. It should be said in passing that, generally speaking, English law makes very slow and painful headway in giving effect to European Community law. The 1968 Convention has as its principal object the making of reciprocal arrangements for recognition and enforcement of awards given in the courts of one Community member cheaper and easier in another Community country. It therefore adds a little more "spice" to the *Mareva* jurisdiction generally so far as EEC members are concerned. Under section 25 of the 1982 Act it is not required as a pre-condition of the granting of a *Mareva* injunction that the *same* court has jurisdiction over the action in respect of which preservation of the asset is sought.

Lord Denning, M.R., had earlier stated in court (see his judgment in the Court of Appeal in *The Siskina*[48]) that *Mareva* jurisdiction should be co-extensive with Article 24 of the 1968 Convention. Article 24 of the Convention reads:

Application may be made to the Court of the Contracting State for such provisional, including protective, measures as may be available under the law of that State, even if under this Convention, the Courts of another Contracting State have jurisdiction as to the substance of the matter.

Now that the 1982 statute is effective in the United Kingdom Lord Denning seems to have been proved correct (not for the first time!).

People who "go after" *Mareva* injunctions can, by doing so, "persuade" a defendant to give security. This is one idea of it – to bring pressure to bear, to hamper, to irritate.

Does it matter whether the defendant is based in or out of the jurisdiction?

Recent court decisions (specifically *dicta* in the *Rasu*[49] case by Lord Denning, M.R., and in *Barclay-Johnson* v. *Yuill*[50]) have made it

48. [1979] A.C. 210.
49. See fn. 44, *supra*.
50. *Barclay-Johnson* v. *Yuill* [1980] 1 W.L.R. 1259.

substantially clear that it is immaterial whether the defendant is himself based inside or outside the jurisdiction though such information may, to a greater or more likely lesser degree, go to influence the judge in the exercising of his discretion. Obviously the crux is – is he, the defendant, likely to remove his assets. If *this* is the crux of the matter, his place of residence is largely, if not entirely, irrelevant. The defendant's personal characteristics are, and rightly should be, *not* a major factor which should influence a judge in the exercise of his discretion. The essence of English courts is that all foreigners, regardless of race, colour or creed, are given equal treatment and consideration if they seek the aid of an English court.

Permanent commitment by way of nationality or domicile or both is, for similar reasons, not a sound factor possibly to dissuade a judge to deny an application for a *Mareva* injunction. So much of trade has an international flavour and it is easy in these enlightened times to "flee the jurisdiction", to transfer bank accounts, now that so many exchange controls have been lifted, at the drop of a hat that what appears permanent may well be only an illusion.

Advantage of Mareva over arrest

It is now time to compare more closely the *Mareva* procedure with arrest of ship (a tangible asset). It is *not* the idea of a *Mareva* injunction to interfere, disproportionately, with the defendant's ability to carry on with his business activities generally.

One distinct advantage of this right over the right *in rem* is that in taking arrest action pursuant to the latter it is not permitted to arrest more than one ship whereas it *is* possible to "*Mareva*" more than one ship (tangible asset(s)) in respect of the same claim. Because of this it is up to the *arrestor* (as opposed to the applicant for an injunction) to take care that the ship which he does eventually arrest is of sufficient value to provide adequate security. He cannot arrest two (or more) to obtain in *aggregate* adequate security. He *may* issue writs against more than one but *service* can only be upon one selected one.

"Ambulatory" effect

It was said in *The Cretan Harmony*[51] that when the injunction refers to a

---

51. *Cretanor Maritime Co. Ltd.* v. *Irish Marine Management Ltd. (The Cretan Harmony)* [1978] 1 Lloyd's Rep. 425.

body of unspecified assets it must be capable of having an ambulatory effect so as to apply to all the assets of the defendant which at any time while the injunction remains "on foot" may be within the jurisdiction . . . "There must, in theory, always at least be a possibility that the charterers may at some time have assets in excess of the value stated in the injunction in which case they would be free to remove any assets representing that excess or a part of it".

In *The Angel Bell*[52] Robert Goff, J., said: "I do not believe that the *Mareva* jurisdiction was intended to rewrite the English law of insolvency".

In *The Angel Bell*[53] he also said:

"Why should a defendant not be free to use his assets to pay his debts if a plaintiff has not yet proceeded to judgment against that defendant but is still in the unprotected and preliminary position of having a claim for an unliquidated sum . . . It does not make commercial sense that a party claiming unliquidated damages should, without himself proceeding to judgment, prevent the defendant from using his assets to satisfy his debts as they fall due and be put in a position of having to allow his creditors to proceed to judgment with consequent loss of credit and of commercial standing".

The Niedersachsen Case[54] – restatement of principles

In the 1983 reported case of *The Niedersachsen* much reaffirmation of the principles took place. The facts involved an attempt by the buyers of the vessel to "*Mareva*" the actual purchase price as soon as it was made over to the sellers so that they, the buyers, would not be left in the position of having an eventual damages award in their favour (potentially) being unsatisfied through lack of assets of the defendant seller, the actual sale proceeds paid to them by the plaintiffs themselves being very likely their only assets within the jurisdiction.

A *Mareva* injunction was granted in the first instance *ex parte* but at an *inter partes* hearing later the injunction was discharged. Again, the court's thinking centred around the minimum requirement that the plaintiff must show that he had a "good arguable case" on the merits. This was described by the appeal judges (to whom the case was eventually referred by the plaintiffs in the hope of getting the decision to lift the injunction overturned) as the "threshold", i.e. the

52. See fn. 42, *supra*.
53. See fn. 42, *supra*.
54. *The Niedersachsen* [1983] 2 Lloyd's Rep. 600.

beginning only, and that the plaintiff was still required to go beyond that and put before the court evidence which the court could then consider as a whole before deciding whether or not to exercise this jurisdiction which is now embodied in section 37 of the Supreme Court Act 1981. The appeal judges reaffirmed also their view that the *Mareva* jurisdiction cannot be invoked "for the purpose of providing plaintiffs with security for claims", even where these appear likely to succeed and even when there is no reason to suppose that an order for an injunction, or the provision of some appropriate security by way of substitute by the defendants would cause any real hardship.

What matters, they said, is not so much a distinction being made between the *object* of the removal of the assets and the *effect* of doing so. That is not the right test to use. The test is and should be – whether, on the assumption that the plaintiffs have shown at least a good arguable case, the court concludes, on the *whole* evidence before it, that a refusal of a *Mareva* injunction would involve a real risk that a judgment or award in favour of the plaintiff would remain unsatisfied.

In the ultimate, they said, if the case appears to the court to be one in which it is "just and convenient" to grant an injunction then it should be done. This accords with what is now the statutory wording (section 37 of the 1981 Act). Judges should also bear well in mind that if, and to the extent that, the granting of a *Mareva* injunction inflicts hardship on the defendant his (the defendant's) legitimate interests must prevail over the plaintiff's who is seeking simply to obtain security for a claim which may appear well founded but which still has to be established at trial.

In the earlier days of *Mareva* jurisdiction the criterion of a "good arguable case" on its own was "on all fours" with the requirements of the court before it granted permission to serve a writ *in personam outside* the jurisdiction (Rules of the Supreme Court, Order 11). But the analogy has dimmed since the *Mareva* jurisdiction has extended its scope to defendants even within the jurisdiction.

In summary of the immediate foregoing, it would be fair to say that the plaintiff must show more than merely a *prima facie* case, indeed more than merely an arguable case, it must be a *good* arguable case. But even that does not mean that the court must place a percentage degree of success on the likely result. To do so would or could be tantamount to the *Mareva* court actually entering into a trial of the issues. The plaintiff does not have to go so far as to convince the judge that he is likely to win.

Casual observers of the use and practice of the *Mareva* injunction might be forgiven for describing it as a "creeping up upon" exercise, a "proceeding by stealth" against an unwary defendant. This is not really justified criticism since an English court will be only too ready to deny an injunction if it considers on the evidence put before it *ex parte* that the plaintiff is doing "just that". They will condemn it as an abuse of the procedure. It is for this very good reason that it is incumbent upon anyone applying *ex parte* for such an injunction that he makes a full and frank disclosure of the facts as he sees or knows them. Failure to do this will likely mean that at any subsequent *inter partes* hearing he will "come a cropper" and the injunction will be lifted (*The Assios*[55]). Set against this reasoning, however, must be the counter thought as already expressed on page 37, that one of the basic purposes of this type of legal manoeuvre is to "get in quick" to prevent a defendant who may have few scruples disposing of his assets within the jurisdiction at the "drop of a hat" which in this "push button" world can mean a "few seconds only". The borderline is thus fine for *Mareva* jurisdiction is not designed merely so that it can be invoked to obtain security for a judgment in advance and still less as a means of pressurizing defendants into settlements (this was made clear by th' court in *Z Ltd.* v. *A-Z*[56]. To use it in circumstances when there may t no real danger of the defendant dissipating his assets so as to mak himself judgment-proof will be an abuse of the system.

How do you obtain a Mareva injunction?

It is essentially, as already emphasized, an *ex parte* application (remember the "creeping up upon" exercise). You must put before the Commercial Court judge (usually you will be represented by a junior counsel) a writ, previously issued, with the bare minimum – inevitably because of the almost certain urgency of your need to obtain such an injunction. The application must be supported by an affidavit which must at its minimum state: (i) the nature of your claim; (ii) its amount; (iii) a bona fide brief statement of whatever counter arguments the defendant may already have put forward; (iv) information regarding the existence, or at least the inference of existence, of assets within the jurisdiction of the *Mareva* court, giving specific particulars, if actually known, for example actual bank

55. *The Assios* [1979] 1 Lloyd's Rep. 331.
56. *Z Ltd.* v. *A-Z* [1982] 1 Lloyd's Rep. 240.

accounts and/or balances therein; (v) evidence of a *real* risk of removal of those assets from the jurisdiction either abroad or dissipated within the jurisdiction itself; (vi) a frank and complete disclosure of any matters of which you, the applicant, are actually aware and which you believe would assist the commercial judge in reaching his decision.

You will be required to give an undertaking supported by security in case your application proves to be unjustified.

Resuming the study of action "in rem" – what of bunkers on board?

When a time-chartered ship is appraised and sold by Admiralty Court order who can claim the proceeds of sale of the bunkers on board at the time? For guidance on answering this question it is worth turning to *The Span Terza*[57] to see how the House of Lords viewed such circumstances under English law. The vessel had been appraised and sold in July 1982 subsequent to an arrest at the suit of the owners of the vessel *Neptunia* who had obtained a judgment in their favour for unpaid hire and wrongful repudiation. The issue for their Lordships to decide was who could claim the proceeds of the sale of the bunkers on board. Subsequent to the order for sale (which was made in December 1981) but prior to the actual sale the charterers of the *Span Terza* had given her owners notice of cancellation of the existing charter-party which they were contractually permitted to do if there had been a continuous off-hire period exceeding 25 days due to an arrest of the vessel.

Whose property was the bunkers? If the owners' property then it was part of the security available to the arrestor. If the charterers' property they and only they were entitled to the proceeds. Who had paid for them? At the time both of the ship's arrest (November 1981) and of the cancellation of the charter five weeks later the charterers had paid for all the bunkers. A small quantity, with which the court was not concerned, was in fact used by the Admiralty Marshal during the arrest period in his capacity as ship's custodian.

As might be expected, the Admiralty judge decided that the answer to the problem pivoted upon the construction of the relevant charter-party. Three propositions were considered: 1. That the

57. *The Span Terza (No. 2)* [1984] 1 Lloyd's Rep. 119 (H.L.).

property in the bunkers vested in the owners as soon as it was delivered to the vessel. This theory was rejected at all judicial levels, the Admiralty judge at first instance, the Court of Appeal, and the House of Lords. All said this was inconsistent with the wording in the relevant clauses and with certain selected words used, for example that the charterers shall *provide* fuel . . . that they shall *take over and pay* for the fuel . . . together with various references to *price*. Unless the charterers acquired title (property) these words would be without meaning. The owners might well have *possession* as *bailees* but possession of in law and property in something are two different concepts.

In 1980 (in *The Saint Anna*[58]) Sheen, J., had (rightly so, said their Lordships) rejected as owners' submission that the property in bunkers vested in the owners merely by virtue of delivery of them to the vessel. (The *Saint Anna* charter-party was a Shelltime 3 form but the terms of it were similar to NYPE.)

Proposition 2 was that a clause in the charter (3) had specified the minimum quantities of fuel and diesel oil to be on board at delivery and redelivery respectively and the scale of prices to be charged applied not only at delivery and redelivery but also in the event of a premature cancellation if rightly exercised by the charterers (allowed under clause 71). Their Lordships did not like this proposition either. They favoured the following theory/proposition: the proximate cause of the cancellation was the remaining of the ship off hire for more than 25 consecutive days *under arrest*. It was immaterial *where* the ship was at the time. Thus, and as the charter contained no clear stipulations as to what should happen to the bunkers in the event of the charterers exercising their option of premature termination, the ordinary rules of law should be applied and these, they said, were the laws of bailment. So long as the charter-party contract subsisted the owners had the right and indeed duty to use the bunkers consistent with their obligations to instruct their master to comply with their duty to allow the charterers to use and employ the ship.

At the time of cancellation this very right to use and consume *itself* ceased together with their contractual rights (as yet unexercised) and duties (as yet unperformed). But the owners remained bailees.

---

58. *The Saint Anna* [1980] 1 Lloyd's Rep. 180.

The practicalities of arrest

What does a writ *in rem* cost? – £55. What does a warrant of arrest cost? – £20. These charges are laid down but readers are warned that they are liable to change and the figures quoted are those ruling at the time of writing. These charges are unavoidable. The arrestor is bound to pay them, or perhaps more accurately, his solicitor will pay them on his behalf. A person, or corporate entity, contemplating making an arrest will, assuming he has a valid claim and that it is a claim entitling him to proceed *in rem*, be required to prove this entitlement on oath.

If service of an arrest warrant is to be done it is done by the Admiralty Marshal in London or by his deputies, who will be Customs officers, in other ports within the jurisdiction (England or Wales). The High Court, geographically situated in London, has "branches" all over the jurisdiction, i.e. all around England and Wales. There are thus District Registries all over the country which can perform the work performed by the Admiralty Registry which itself is situated in the Royal Courts of Justice building in London. These District Registries can issue arrest warrants but once issued all arrests are procedurally channelled through the Marshal in London and the warrant can only actually be served through his good offices.

We have so far referred to the unavoidable and fixed charges. Beyond that it is largely a question of which solicitors the arrestor chooses to represent him in his problem of taking legal action. One thing which the solicitor will have to provide to the Admiralty Marshal on the arrestor's behalf is a satisfactory undertaking, usually personal by the solicitor, that he will pay on demand the fees and expenses of the Marshal in connection with the arrest and custody of the vessel. This must necessarily be an "open-ended" guarantee since nobody knows at the time of demand what the Marshal's eventual out-of-pocket expenses will be. They may be heavy or light depending on the length of time the vessel is detained under arrest before being released on provision or suitable alternative security or sold by order of the court.

That custodial expenses can range widely according to individual circumstances is illustrated, for example, by the possibility that if a vessel is under arrest for more than a brief space the port authority may insist that she be moved to a different berth, thus incurring shifting expenses.

A shipowner may take a little time to muster the appropriate security sufficient to provide a satisfactory guarantee for the claim, plus interest and costs up to the value of the seized ship. This, so far as P. & I. type claims are concerned, would depend on how popular the shipowner is with his P. & I. Club since a P. & I. Club letter of undertaking is a very common form of security put up and is recognized and respected over much of the world but not as yet universally. If the security demanded is a bank guarantee this may take longer to arrange. Also a bail bond can be provided to the court, though this is not so common as it used to be. Under a bail bond the court is empowered to "call it in", whereas the other types of security aforementioned are given personally to the claimant who would eventually have to bring an action under the guarantee if the guarantor subsequently showed reluctance to honour it in accordance with its terms. Whatever the nature of security being sought the arrestor must be reasonable in his demands.

Anybody who fears that by taking arrest action within English jurisdiction he exposes himself to an unpalatable counter suit for wrongful arrest may dismiss his fears. Although naturally a cause of action for wrongful arrest potentially does lie within English law, the practical fact is that it is hardly ever pursued. You have to prove gross negligence or malice to establish wrongful arrest. This is very rare, if ever. Excessive demands for security will not be tolerated and the owners will be keen to release their ship from arrest anyway. The affidavit requirements which must support an application for an arrest warrant should also effectively, to a very large extent, nullify the likelihood that the wrong ship will have been selected for seizure.

It would probably not be far from the truth to venture the comment that English jurisdiction may be the cheapest place in which to effect an arrest. The underlying reason for this is probably not so much to encourage "big business" for the Admiralty Court but rather an admission that the English courts, whether Admiralty or otherwise, should be freely accessible (and this would include being accessible at reasonably low cost) to all who seek their aid, whether resident within the jurisdiction or foreign to it.

Whether it is better for a plaintiff to take proceedings *in personam* or *in rem* is a matter for his own personal choice. Admiralty law and procedure gives him the choice. He had best consult his solicitor for guidance (preferably, of course, one versed in Admiralty law). One factor which will probably influence such a decision is the inability to serve a writ *in rem outside* the jurisdiction of the court issuing the writ whereas, in certain circumstances (as permitted by Order 11, rules 1 and 2 of the Rules of the Supreme Court) a court *may* permit service of a writ *in personam* outside the jurisdiction. The jurisdiction (i.e. the court's power) to give such leave would be likely to be exercised in favour of the originator of the summons and complaint if the complaint was genuine, there were triable issues of fact, the complaint was neither malicious nor frivolous, etc.

The issuing of a writ *in rem* requires the attendance of the plaintiff's solicitor or, if he is suing as an individual, himself, at the Royal Courts of Justice or at a District Registry in the provinces. Three or more copies of a writ are required. The fees are paid for in cash on the spot whether it is in London or a District Registry. The writ must be endorsed with a brief statement of the nature of the claim.

No warrant of arrest may be issued until there has been an issue of a writ, though it is not necessary that the latter has been served.

In the Admiralty Registry in London is kept a "caveat" book where all caveats are registered. When issuing a warrant you are obliged to make a search for caveats. Even if a caveat against arrest is entered in respect of the particular ship selected for arrest, this does not prevent arrest. The plaintiff can go ahead but does so at his peril. Caveats *against arrest* are, however, rare these days.

To release a ship from arrest a document has to be filed in the Registry. It is also necessary to obtain the agreement of the plaintiff and all caveators. The Admiralty Marshal then instructs the release of the vessel and sends his messenger to do so. Caveats *against release* are quite common by persons with claims *in rem* against the same ship. Broadly speaking, they entitle the caveator to notice of any proposed release so that he can arrest the vessel himself if he so wishes, thus putting himself in the position of having issued a warrant. This is particularly popular procedure in matters of bankruptcy. At the time of writing entering a caveat against release costs only £2, considerably cheaper than the costs of taking original arrest action.

The Federal Republic of Germany

Corresponding to the decrease in international trade and transport the number of arrested vessels in West Germany seems to have been reduced constantly over the last five years. Nevertheless, this subject is of high interest and importance for all shipowners as well as their creditors and can recover its previous actuality for each of them every day.

Each case requires conscientious preparation and work under high time pressure and with great responsibility for all parties concerned. The legal proceedings arising from the arrest may last over years and raise interesting questions of high economic importance. The following contribution gives a general outline on the preconditions of the arrest and the proceedings leading to the actual attachment of the vessel, as well as the usual procedure to lift the arrest or terminate the lawsuit.

For the creditor and his lawyer who are looking for suitable security for an open claim against the shipowner, a seagoing vessel in a German port is an object with advantages on the one hand and disadvantages on the other. For claims against a company with only temporary strain on liquidity the arrest is a sharp and effective weapon to obtain another security in exchange. The owners will endeavour to avoid any demurrage or off-hire, the usual consequences of the arrest. On the other hand, if the vessel is without employment and perhaps unsaleable the arrest may remain without effect on the owners and leave them apathetic towards their liabilities. In this case the creditor may have to undergo long and complicated civil proceedings with considerable cost risks and uncertain result. Even a final judgment against the owners and judicial auction may not help him and leave a nasty after-taste and the unhappy feeling to have thrown a lot of good money after bad.

At the beginning of the proceedings it is very often virtually impossible to anticipate which of the two alternatives will come out at the end. Nevertheless, the creditor has to act since the only fact which he knows for certain is that inactivity will leave him alone with his unpaid claim for ever.

51

German flag owners

If a vessel flies the German flag an arrest in Germany will only exceptionally be necessary. Since the owners have to be of German nationality or under the control of German management (body corporate) or management *and* shareholders (partnership) before arresting the vessel a creditor may seize other domestic assets of the owner, for example garnishee freight claims against shippers or agents or bank accounts. Upon the owners' default of payment he may as well register a mortgage in the register of ships or of land titles with the court's help. An arrest of a vessel will only become necessary if these items of property cannot be found or are charged beyond the limit of encumbrances or if the debtor is a one-ship company, the vessel only calling exceptionally at a German port.

Foreign flag owners – implementation of the 1952 Convention on Arrest

In the majority of arrest cases, however, foreign shipowners and their vessels registered outside the Federal Republic of Germany are involved.

Since April 1973 the Federal Republic of Germany has been a member of the Brussels Arrest Convention of 1952. The purpose of this Convention is to restrict the possibilities of arrest with regard to seagoing vessels flying the flag of a contracting State. Therefore the arrest is only allowed for maritime claims against the vessel or against sister ships belonging to the same owners. Maritime claims are specified exclusively in Article 1 of the Convention. Other claims can only be secured if the vessel's home port is situated in a non-contracting State.

Apart from these restrictions resulting from the Convention and of importance only for its members, all kinds of claims can be secured by an arrest and there is no need to prove a connection with the operation of the vessel. A guarantee given by the owners for a subsidiary company or other principal debtor is as suitable as a claim resulting from the purchase of the ship or any other goods by the owners. Only claims for "goods or materials" supplied to a ship for her operation or maintenance are acknowledged as "maritime claims" in Article 1(1)(*k*) of the Convention.

Needless to say, a claim, in order to be secured, must not be time-barred and in the creditor's self-critical opinion be free from other successful objections of the owners.

Shipowners' personal liability

The arrest can only be applied for if the shipowner is personally liable for the creditor's claim. This precondition can raise considerable problems for the applicant if a vessel is owned by a one-ship company flying a flag of convenience and registered in State A, managed however by another company with place of residence in one of the business centres in State B. In this case the court has to be convinced that company B had power of attorney to act for the shipowner or that the master made use of his legal authority to act for the owners, for example signing a bunker requisition or an order form for goods or materials or a repair contract enabling the vessel to proceed on her voyage. The shipowner, not being the debtor himself, it might be sufficient for the creditor's purposes if he guaranteed the claim or is subject to legal liability.

Since the German judge who has to decide the application for the arrest will not know the foreign law stating the legal liability, the creditor is well advised to produce a legal opinion of a well-known law firm with international reputation and experience, disclosing the reasons why the shipowner is personally liable or has the duty to tolerate the attachment of his vessel for the obligations of a third party.

Examples (supply of bunkers, change of ownership)

Typically, this situation has to be faced if the vessel was under time charter or belonged to other owners when the maritime claim arose. Bunkers, for example, are very often ordered by the master or an agent on behalf of unknown charterers. In this case a creditor should produce a perfect bunker requisition signed by the master, in addition to the charterer's order or other documentary evidence showing the joint and several liability of the owners. For cargo claims constituted by the charterers, the Hague Rules may support the creditor's view and hold available a guideline for the German judge.

After the vessel's sale the laws of some countries impose joint and several liability for the seller's debt on the new owners, even if a maritime lien for the creditor's claim is not in existence and the memorandum of agreement does not contain an assumption of liability or collateral promise. If the seller was a one-ship company who remained without any assets after the vessel's sale, the German judge will likely be inclined to accept the new owners' liability for an unpaid maritime claim originating from the operation of the vessel before the date of the memorandum of agreement.

Duty of creditor to declare his motives for taking arrest action

As a second provision for obtaining an arrest order the creditor has to give evidence why he cannot wait for a judgment in ordinary civil proceedings before the competent court. The best example would be if the debtor prepares to leave the country and his liabilities behind him. Mortgaging property beyond the limit of encumbrances, concealment of assets, fraudulent business practices against the creditor or even operations resulting in a heavy loss over a considerable period may also be sufficient. On the other hand, deterioration of assets, imminent danger of bankruptcy or enforcement measures of other creditors will not be accepted. The judge has absolute discretionary jurisdiction and it is nearly impossible to anticipate his requirements to the applicant in this respect.

It is quite obvious that a claimant who wants to arrest a vessel in a German port normally will not be in a position to deliver evidence for one of the aforementioned circumstances and facts out of his debtor's sphere. He can only assure that the shipowner did not meet his financial obligations or undertakings of payment and does not own any assets in Germany, except the vessel expected at or berthed in the German port.

In this situation, section 917(2) of the German Code of Civil Procedure holds available a statutory presumption in favour of the creditor. Sufficient reason for an arrest is in existence if the judgment obtained in ordinary proceedings has to be enforced in a foreign country because of the absence of assets in Germany. Almost 100% of foreign ship arrests are granted by German courts because of this special reason.

As an important exception to this rule the courts will dismiss an application if the shipowner runs a regular scheduled service calling at German ports. In this case the creditor has the opportunity to garnishee the shipowner's claims against his agents and other third party debtors and is not entitled to disturb the operation of the shipping line by an arrest of one of its vessels. In 1981 a Court of Appeal in Hamburg underlined this tendency in the following case: The shipowner was under the control of the government of an African State which constantly shipped coffee to Germany and for this purpose maintained normal business relations over the years with his agent in Hamburg. For every southbound vessel sailing from Hamburg within a three or four-week period, the agent collected freights of more than U.S.$100,000. The court held that the creditor could garnishee these freight claims after ordinary proceedings and was not dependent on the arrest of one of the foreign vessels because in the court's opinion the African government would not discontinue the business relations with the Hamburg agent in order to evade the creditor's claim of only U.S.$35,000.[1]

Unfortunately, we have contradictory judgments of German Courts of Appeal whether the necessity of enforcement outside Germany in the absence of other assets can only be deemed as a sufficient reason for arrest if future judgments of *German* courts shall be secured. Some courts hold that this statutory presumption does not apply if foreign courts have jurisdiction on the merits. In many charter-parties or other international contracts the jurisdiction clause refers any dispute exclusively to courts outside Germany, which leads to the unique result that the arrest of vessels, because of claims arising out of such contracts, would be almost impossible in Germany. Furthermore, foreign shipowners who refuse to accept the jurisdiction of German courts in the bills of lading signed on their behalf would be given preference over German shipowners who cannot protect themselves against the danger of arrest of their vessels in Germany and abroad. As far as shipowners within the EEC are concerned this discrimination has to be considered as a violation of Articles 7 and 76 of the EEC Convention. Furthermore, the supporters of the distinction between German and foreign judgments cannot explain why it is generally agreed upon in German commentaries and court of appeal judgments that the special reason for an arrest provided for in section

1. Judgment of 12.2.1981 (6 U 150/80).

917(2) of the Code of Civil Procedure is available if the claim on the merits is subject to arbitration, irrespective of the seat of the arbitration tribunal being in or outside Germany. Finally, it may also happen that the creditor applies for the arrest of a vessel in Germany after having obtained a judgment of the foreign court in his favour. There can be no doubt that the court has to sustain such a motion and it is hard to understand why the application to secure a future judgment should be decided in a different way.

Reciprocal arrangements

For the aforementioned reasons other German courts are of the legitimate opinion that the benefit of section 917(2) of the Code of Civil Procedure has to be given to all applicants for an arrest even if foreign courts have exclusive jurisdiction on the merits, provided only that the shipowner does not own other assets in Germany. They also hold that the EEC Convention on Jurisdiction and the Enforcement of Judgments in Civil and Commercial Matters 1968 does not prevent a member of the State A securing his claim in his country and proceeding on the merits before the courts of State B, who have exclusive jurisdiction because of the debtor's place of residence. A binding judgment by the Federal Court of Justice to these contradictory opinions is still outstanding.[2]

Practicalities of arrest

Provided the creditor's claim and a sufficient reason why the arrest should be granted are in existence, the application can be filed. It has to contain the applicant's full name and address as well as the names of the directors who are authorized to his representation. A written power of attorney should also be enclosed.

The competent court depends on the claim amount and will normally be the local court or the provincial court of the vessel's port of destination. Only exceptionally the dispute will have been submitted already to another German court who in that case also is competent to grant the arrest. The creditor should be represented by a lawyer, although this is not compulsory. The application has to be made in writing and the German language must be used, but the courts in Hamburg, Bremen and other seaports with overseas or

2. See footnote 6.

international connections will also accept the documents supporting the claim in English.

Preparing his application, the creditor has to anticipate if the merits of the case will reasonably be doubted by the judges and later on contested by the debtor. Any fact at issue has to be provable by documents or by a witness who signs a certificate of affidavit.

Mostly the court decides the application without a hearing. Otherwise the owners or their agents would be informed about the imminent arrest and be enabled to instruct the master not to call at the scheduled port of destination.

If in the court's opinion the petition has no merits it will be dismissed and the creditor can appeal against this judgment. Usually the presiding judge will inform the creditor's lawyer about his objections and give him the opportunity either to complete his arguments or to withdraw the application.

Provision of alternative security

If the court is prepared to sustain the motion the judges have to decide freely after a due assessment of the circumstances if the creditor has to provide a security before the arrest is granted or enforced. There is a mutual effect between valid reasons for the arrest and the kind and amount of security. The reason lies in a specific feature of German arrest law: If, later on, the arrest turns out to be unjustified from the beginning, section 945 of the Code of Civil Procedure awards a claim for damages to the debtor. Such a claim is not restricted to fraudulent misrepresentation or other criminal conduct of the applicant. He is not protected from his opponent's claim if he acted in good faith and obtained the arrest by a court's error in his favour.

The security to be assessed in the arrest order is a guarantee for this claim for damages theoretically arising from the enforcement of every arrest. Only exceptionally the judges will refrain from a security, if, for example, the creditor's solvency is beyond any doubt and the arrest is well founded and almost certainly unappealable. Usually the court asks for a deposit in cash covering the estimated loss of profit which the debtor will suffer while his assets or goods are under arrest. For a vessel her charter rate for the off-hire period due to the arrest will be a fair guideline, restricted however at the beginning of the proceedings by the estimated time which is necessary for the owners to replace the arrest by other appropriate security, for example a bank guarantee or a club letter. A bank guarantee will normally also be accepted as creditor's security.

The court may also increase the original amount of security upon the debtor's appeal. With the arrest order the judges will establish a certain amount which can be deposited by the debtor in order to lift the arrest without the creditor's consent. This amount covers the creditor's claim, including interest and costs and can also be replaced by a guarantee of a major German bank with the creditor's or the court's approval.

Enforcement of arrest

Having obtained the arrest order the creditor will endeavour to enforce it without delay. A court's registrar or the bailiff are responsible for the enforcement of the arrest upon a separate application. To attach a foreign vessel the creditor will instruct the bailiff who visits the vessel, mostly under police attendance, and fixes a chain at her wheel as a symbol for the arrest. More important is the information of the port authorities who will prevent the vessel from sailing as long as the arrest is in existence.

The enforcement of an arrest is not allowed after the beginning of the voyage and outside German ports. The previous legal situation, forbidding the arrest upon the vessel's readiness to sail, was changed in 1973 when Germany became a member of the Arrest Convention.

The arrest order becomes invalid within one month after its delivery to the creditor and hence he is not allowed to enforce it any more. Finally, he has to make sure that service of the arrest to the debtor's address is effected or at least applied for within one week after the attachment of the vessel and within the one-month period mentioned before. Non-observation of these two time limits will also lead to the extinction of the arrest.

Until the enforcement the master and the shipowner usually do not have any knowledge of the arrest. Now there are two ways to proceed.

Procedures when jurisdiction of arrest and jurisdiction "on the merits" are in conflict

(a) Upon request, the vessel's P. & I. Club will hold available a letter of undertaking which will be offered to the creditor in exchange for the arrest. Although he is not bound to accept a security not approved by the court he will usually do so, provided the wording of the club letter enables him to collect his money without further difficulties as soon as judgment on the merits has been issued in his favour. Naturally, the place of jurisdiction and the applicable law are of high importance and points for tough negotiations. Whereas the creditor will endeavour to improve his position and perhaps compel his opponents into a more favourable court, the owners will not yield to this pressure and insist on the original place of jurisdiction. Vessels flying the flag of a contracting State of the Arrest Convention are in a strong position in this respect. Article 7 tries to impede "forum shopping", which very often was the secret purpose behind the arrest of a vessel in a German port. First, the arrest prevented the ship from sailing and in the second place the creditor instituted proceedings on the merits, holding that German courts were competent as *forum rei sitae* notwithstanding the fact that they did not have jurisdiction without the arrest. The Convention does not approve such endeavours and provides a solution for different places of arrest and jurisdiction on the merits.

By an arrest against a vessel flying a flag of a non-contracting State the creditor may still try to establish a forum more convenient than the home court of the vessel or the jurisdiction clause in the charter-party or basic contract. Recently German courts have however practised substantial obstruction against this policy, even apart from the Convention.

(b) If no agreement about a club letter or other guarantee is reached the owners may decide to appeal against the arrest order. The court who granted the arrest will then fix a hearing and deal with the case again. Owners and their opponents may submit pleadings and witnesses may appear and be heard. Both preconditions for the arrest, the creditor's claim as well as the reason why he could not wait for judgment in ordinary proceedings, may be in dispute again and if no settlement can be achieved with the court's help the judges have either to dismiss the appeal or lift the arrest. They are also allowed to cancel, reduce or increase their initial judgment with respect to the security required from the creditor. It may even be established higher than the claim amount and in that case the creditor will probably lose interest in the further maintenance of the arrest.

The judgment delivered after the hearing is subject to a second appeal. It has to be lodged within one month after service of the written judgment to the losing party and reasons can be given within another month. Because of the high risk connected with long-lasting arrest proceedings for the shipowner as well as for his opponents, neither of them should take full advantage of these time limits and should do the utmost to obtain a final judgment of the Court of Appeal in a shorter period.

(c) There is no alternative between the steps described under (a) and (b). On the contrary, if the owners are convinced that they have good reasons for an appeal, they should nevertheless offer appropriate security. The creditor is also well advised to accept such an offer even if he feels that the owners' appeal will remain without success. Such an interim agreement minimizes the risk of off-hire claims or other damages following out of the arrest and does not have prejudice in favour or against the legal position of one of the parties.

TIME LIMIT

(d) Having been informed about the arrest order and even before its enforcement, the shipowner may apply for a time limit to be set against the creditor within which the action leading to a judgment on the merits of the case must be brought. This authority is expressively laid down in Article 7(2) of the Arrest Convention corresponding to section 926 of the Code of Civil Procedure. Non-observance of this time limit enables the debtor to lift the arrest.

German commentaries hold a different view whether the creditor complies with the time limit by an action before a foreign court. For some of them foreign litispendence is only equivalent if the foreign judgment will be acknowledged in Germany. In the field of the Arrest Convention this opinion conflicts with Article 7(3) and, generally speaking, the acknowledgement of the foreign judgment should not be taken as a precondition for the maintenance of the arrest. The contradictory opinion would mean that the creditor is forced to bring an action in Germany which has to be dismissed for formal reasons if foreign courts have exclusive jurisdiction on the merits. Apart from this, it is in the creditor's own interest to bring the action before the German court who granted the arrest. These judges issued an unappealable preliminary judgment in his favour and he avoids eventual difficulties with the future acknowledgment of the foreign judgment by the German courts.

Judicial sale

The realization of the security obtained by the arrest, i.e. the judicial sale of the vessel, cannot be described in detail. There is no exception to the rule that the creditor must have obtained a judgment for his claim, either final or at least provisionally enforceable. Even a strong decline in prices or an exceptionally good offer for the vessel do not justify a premature auction without an enforceable judgment on the merits. It was recently adjudged by a Hamburg court that a provision of the Code of Civil Procedure, allowing the sale of movables under arrest in order to avoid a considerable loss in value or inproportionate charges for custody, does not apply to the sale of an arrested vessel.

As mentioned before, a foreign judgment is not sufficient to institute a judicial sale. Even if the EEC Convention on Jurisdiction and the Enforcement of Judgments in Civil and Commercial Matters 1968 applies or the enforcement and acknowledgement of the foreign judgment is guaranteed otherwise, the creditor has to undergo separate acknowledgement proceedings before the auction may begin. Although summary proceedings take place for this purpose and the German judge is not allowed to deal with the merits of the case again the law holds available wide-ranging objections for a shipowner who wants to delay the loss of his vessel. Therefore a creditor who wants to realize his security by judicial sale should make sure before the beginning of the arrest proceedings that a claim on the merits is admissible in Germany. If it is prohibited by an exclusive jurisdiction clause establishing the competence of foreign courts he should start to have the foreign judgment acknowledged in Germany as soon as possible.

Maritime liens

Only in a public auction the creditor who arrested the vessel eventually has to fight against maritime liens which may have preference over his claim.

Germany abolished maritime liens for cargo claims arising out of charter-parties or other contracts in 1973 and since then provides this form of security only for the members of the crew with regard to outstanding wages, etc., port, pilot and salvage charges, general average contributions and, finally, damage claims as the result of collision. These liens are subject to a one-year prescription and in this field the creditor can calculate his risk to some extent. More difficult is the appraisal of maritime liens originating from foreign ports. German commentaries hold controversial views to the applicable law with regard to the creation of maritime liens outside German territorial waters. Most of them recommend the law of the flag or the law which rules the claim itself (*lex causae*). The acknowledgement of foreign maritime liens is even more in dispute. This question has to be decided by German law as *lex fori* and it seems fair that maritime liens equivalent to those admitted in Germany shall have equal rank and precedence over all other security rights, including ship mortgages. What should happen, however, to contractual liens arising, for example, from a bunker delivery to a vessel in a port in the United States for which German law, as stated above, would not grant a maritime lien to the supplier? In my opinion the German judge should acknowledge the foreign security with priority over foreign mortgages, giving precedence, however, to claims which are secured by maritime liens in Germany as well as in the foreign country. Recent court judgments on this problem have not been published and it is difficult to anticipate how the first case will be decided.

Summarizing, it can be stated that the judicial sale of an arrested vessel can hold available a lot of unpleasant surprises for the creditor because of the possible priority of foreign mortgages and maritime liens.

Possibility of wrongful arrest

The debtor's claim for damages because of wrongful arrest has already been mentioned. The creditor is liable for any damages which the shipowner suffers from the enforcement of the arrest, regardless of his personal fault. The only precondition is that the arrest was unjustified from the beginning. It is quite obvious that considerable sums may mount up even in a couple of days following the arrest of a seagoing vessel.

This "boomerang" of the arrest is even more dangerous for the creditor because some courts are of the opinion that the judgment lifting the arrest on the debtor's appeal in the arrest proceedings has binding authority over the judge who has to decide the damages case. Out of this opinion follows the logical consequence that the creditor cannot defend himself against the shipowners' claim sufficiently, even more an unfair disadvantage because in the arrest proceedings, as stated above, there are only two stages of appeal, whereas normal actions exceeding the amount of DM.40,000 have access to the Federal Court of Justice who may only refuse to deal with the appeal if the case is not of fundamental importance. Hopefully, this court will correct the theory of the binding authority in the near future following those commentators who already are of the opinion that a shipowner claiming for damage because of wrongful arrest has to give evidence for the error in the arrest order just as for all other facts of his case.[3] A presumption in his favour based on the judgment annulling the arrest order cannot be accepted.

A claim for wrongful arrest does not, however, depend on such a reversal of the arrest order. The shipowner may also leave the arrest unappealed and institute proceedings because of wrongful arrest based on the declaration that the court granted the arrest by error. The local and international jurisdiction for this action lies with the court who granted the arrest. In the absence of litispendence before another court or a judgment on the merits for the claim secured by the arrest, the creditor may put forward a counterclaim. An interesting question arises if an exclusive international jurisdiction exists for the claim against the shipowner. Is a counterclaim admissable before a German court in this case or is the creditor at least entitled to set off? In my opinion this question has to be answered in the affirmative since any other solution would mean an unfair discrimination of the creditor, allowing the shipowner not only to derive unjustified benefit from the arrest but also to evade his creditors once more. A Federal Court judgment on this problem is also outstanding.[4]

The creditor may raise different objections against the claim for wrongful arrest. He may argue that the owners performed necessary repairs to maintain the vessel's class or claim relief by reason of other advantages following out of the arrest for the owners. He may also set up the defence that owners provoked the arrest or did not bring to his knowledge an extraordinary amount or likelihood of damage. Another defence may result from the circumstances of the individual.

Similar proceedings

Finally, some particulars of the German arrest law should be mentioned.

3. See footnote 6.
4. *Ibid.*

(a) Whereas claims for payment are secured by an arrest order the security for all other claims can be obtained by an interlocutory injunction. If, for example, a shipowner flying the German flag promised to register a mortgage in favour of a bank or another creditor and prepared a sale of his vessel before doing so, the bank may obtain security by a judgment. An interesting case was decided by the Hamburg Court of Appeal in 1981.[5] During negotiations about his claim against the shipowner the creditor had promised not to arrest the vessel after having reached an intermediary settlement. A dispute arose later about the inadequacy of this settlement. The creditor announced an arrest and the shipowner applied for an injunction forbidding the creditor the enforcement of any arrest. The court sustained this motion. From the written reasons of the judgment it appears that the injunction does not only prevent the enforcement of an arrest in Germany but wherever the vessel calls at a port world-wide.

Another Hamburg court refused the shipowner's application in a similar case some years ago. In that case the creditor had also threatened to attach the vessel, but was not obliged to refrain from the arrest by contractual relations. The owners tried to establish such an obligation based on the allegation that the creditor's claim was without merits, just as they were entitled under German law to file an action for a declaratory judgment stating that the creditor's claim did not exist. The court held, rightly, that this peculiar form of action was not admissible in arrest proceedings and the owners were sufficiently protected by the remedies provided for by the German and foreign arrest law.

Interlocutory injunctions have also been issued by German labour courts in favour of the crew because of outstanding wages and violation of German law or international Conventions relating to safety on board ship. In addition, the public authorities responsible for the control of these regulations have certain powers to arrest, detain or otherwise prevent the vessel's sailing or impose other prohibitions. Disputes involving public law are, however, not decided by the civil courts and therefore are beyond the subject of this chapter.

(b) There is another form of protection for shipowners against an arrest of their vessel in German ports. If they fear an attachment they may deliver pleadings containing their defence to any court having jurisdiction over the port of destination. Their petition will be not to

5. Judgment of 22.1.1981 (6 U 171/80).

arrest the vessel or at least fix a hearing before an arrest is granted and to make its enforcement dependent on high security of the applicant. The owners, having been informed already about the danger of arrest, there is no reason not to hear both parties before the case is decided. Therefore most judges will sustain the motion of the owners and decide the case only after a hearing. This form of protection was adopted from the law of unfair competition and introduced into arrest cases only recently.

(c) If the shipowner is of German nationality and becomes insolvent immediately after the arrest the creditor has to face the danger that the receiver will contest the legal position obtained in the arrest proceedings. German bankruptcy law determines the conditions for such an action of the receiver. In brief it will only be successful if he proves that the arrest was obtained after or 10 days before the stoppage of payments or the shipowner's application for bankruptcy, the creditor having knowledge of these circumstances.

The creditor will have the same attitude towards this danger of losing the fruits of his efforts as he has to the whole arrest procedure: Inactivity and overestimating this danger means permanent loss of his money, instituting the arrest proceedings means the chance to obtain security and finally satisfaction. He should therefore not hesitate to take the necessary steps.[6]

---

6. Whilst this book was in course of printing, the Federal Court by order of 8.1.1985 (VI ZR 145/83) refused to hear an appeal on the pros and cons of the questions mentioned under footnotes 2, 3 and 4. Hence the highest German civil court is of the opinion that:

(a) the creditor is liable without personal negligence for any damages resulting from the arrest, provided only the judge who has to decide the damages case is convinced of the erroneous application of section 917(2) of the Code of Civil Procedure in the creditor's favour in the arrest order;

(b) this judge is bound to a previous judgment lifting the arrest for this reason upon the shipowner's appeal;

(c) the original arrest claim, subject to exclusive foreign jurisdiction, cannot be set off against the shipowner's claim for wrongful arrest.

The international shipping world will hardly show sympathy for these strange results of German legislation and/or jurisdiction. They throw a strong light on the fact that an international arrest law does not exist and that German national law has not been properly adjusted to the 1952 Convention on Arrest, although Germany became a member in 1973. Hopefully the contracting States will agree on the necessary amendments in the near future and at least the members of the EC will ratify such a unified arrest law including the preconditions and consequences of wrongful arrest. Otherwise the goal of the Convention will not be reached and it has to be anticipated that the misunderstandings mentioned in the first lines of this book will rather grow than disappear.

Japan

TAMEYUKI HOSOI

Introduction

Japan's Civil Procedure Act 1890, as amended, and the Civil Execution Act 1979 provide for three different ways by which a ship can be arrested, as follows:

(1) Provisional arrest

This is a procedure to arrest a ship in order to secure in advance a claimant's probable claim against a shipowner, i.e. the merit of the case should later be decided by a court in Japan or another country. If no merit is eventually found by the court, the arrested ship must be released. As this procedure gives the claimant the right to arrest the ship only temporarily, as security for his probable but not yet finally admitted claim, no actual sale by auction will automatically follow, and if a counter-security is put up by the opponent side, i.e. the debtor, who is usually the shipowner, the vessel can be released.

(2) Compulsory execution

This is a procedure by which to execute one's firm claim, which has already been admitted by the court, against a ship as the debtor's property, allowing the claimant to recover his claim. This procedure naturally leads to the actual sale of the arrested ship, unless the debtor puts up a counter-security. A foreign court judgment and a foreign arbitration award can also be executed in Japan against a ship when she calls at a Japanese port, subject to a Japanese court's recognition.

(3) Public auction without a judgment

A mortgaged right, maritime lien and possessory lien enable a claimant to arrest a concerned ship which will subsequently be sold by public auction. The advantage in this procedure is that the claimant does not have to put up a deposit with the court before he can initiate the proceedings.

In all the above ways, a writ can be served on her master as he is considered to be the statutory authoritative agent for the owners when she is away from her registered port. A sister ship may also be arrested, except in the case of an application for arrest based on maritime lien.

Maritime lien

Maritime lien enables a claimant to arrest and sell a ship by court auction, the proceeds of which are paid into a monetary fund, from which a claimant can receive the amount of his claim. Under Japanese law, maritime lien rights always supersede mortgage rights, and there is no distinction between mortgages such as preferred mortgage, and others.

Under Japanese law, the following claims are given maritime lien:

(1) Expenses relating to the sale of the ship and her appurtenances by public auction, and the expenses of preservation after the commencement of the proceedings for the sale by public auction.

(2) Expenses of preservation of the ship and her appurtenances at the last port.

(3) All public dues levied on the ship in respect of the voyage.

(4) Pilotage and towage.

(5) Salvage award and the ship's contribution to general average.

(6) Claims which have arisen from the necessity for the continuance of the voyage.

(7) Claims of the master and other mariners which have arisen from their contracts of employment.

(8) Claims which have arisen from the commercial sale, construction, or equipment of the ship, in cases where the ship has not yet made any voyage after her sale or construction; and claims in respect of the equipment and food and bunkers of the ship for her last voyage.

(9) Cargo claim rights provided by Article 19 of Japan's International Carriage of Goods by Sea Act 1957.

(10) Claim rights which may be limited by Japan's Limitation of Shipowners Liability Act 1975, as amended in 1982.

Supply of bunkers possibly gives rise to maritime lien either in item (6) or (8) above, as may be the case.

"Her last voyage" in item (8) above does not necessarily mean the physically and historically last voyage leading to the end of a ship's life. A reputable scholar indicates that "her last voyage" is the last voyage of a certain series of voyages in a commercial unit or circle. This should be developed in more detail by court cases and analyses thereof.

Among the above maritime lien rights, superiority is in principle given in the above order. In practice, many of the above-listed maritime lien related items are initially paid by a ship's or a charterer's local agent. Such a local agent is now usually considered to be entitled to reimbursement from the ship's interests by virtue of maritime lien. However, the fee for the agent's services is not all the time admitted by the court to give rise to a maritime lien.

Many of the above maritime lienable rights time-bar one year after they arise, although the claims themselves will, as the case may be, continue past the first year without being accompanied by liens.

In the case of arrest of a vessel based on a maritime lien, only the particular vessel against which a claim was made may be arrested, and no sister ship may be arrested. Sister ships may be arrested by means of provisional arrest.

A claimant need not lodge any deposit with the court nor its agency, other than for court costs, revenue stamps or the like, which are usually nominal. This is one of the most advantageous schemes favouring a claimant.

Maritime lien recognized by the law of the country where the principal claim was created and simultaneously by the law of the flag of the vessel to be arrested is also likely to be recognized subject to circumstances, even if Japanese substantive law does not recognize such a lien. This on the one hand favours a claimant, since he can arrest a ship even by virtue of a foreign orientated claim, which may not be admitted to give rise to a lien under Japanese law. On the other hand, however, this would, as may be the case, work against a claimant if, for instance, a principal claim gives rise to a maritime lien in the country where the claim arose, but such a claim is not recognized to be a maritime lienable right by the law of the country whose flag she carries, or vice versa.

An application for the arrest of a ship by a claimant is occasionally accepted and admitted by the court without hearing any defences from the shipowner or her charterer, and it takes some time for the shipowner to have her released by putting up counter-security with the court, etc. If a shipowner is worried that his ship will probably be arrested in Japanese territorial waters without being given a reasonable time in advance to check and inspect the accuracy and/or genuineness of claim vouchers or the like (this feature is more likely to occur when the ship is time chartered, in which case the shipowner usually has no immediate and direct access to the contents of the claim as the claim is often made on the order of the time charterer through its local agent), the shipowner is able to apply for a special court order to restrain such a claimant from arresting a ship, by submitting a sufficient reason and a counter-security to the court beforehand.

Possessory lien

A dockyard, for example, is usually entitled to keep a ship which was equipped and/or repaired in the dockyard until the equipment/repair charges are paid, even if such charges do not fall within the above maritime lienable rights. If the shipowner is for some reason unable to settle the claim, the dockyard may proceed with sale of the ship by public auction supervised by the court as long as the ship remains in the custody of the dockyard. If the ship leaves the dockyard, the possessory lien vanishes.

Mortgage

Not only Japanese mortgage, but also foreign mortgage on a foreign flag ship, can usually be executed in Japan.

Types of claims

A ship can be arrested for any type of monetary claim against the owner. The claim need not necessarily have fallen due; a claim subject to a condition precedent, a claim subject to time and even a surety's right of future possible indemnification against the principal obligor are in advance allowed as claims for the purposes of provisional arrest (so far as it is evidently shown that unless an arrest is ordered at this stage the future enforcement of the claim may be endangered).

Since a later increase of the claim amount may meet some difficulty if the limitation of action expires before such an increase, it is in many cases advisable that the claim be set out in the maximum possible amount.

Evidence of existence of a claim

(1) Provisional arrest

It is only necessary to show the court the probability of a valid claim in order to secure arrest as a provisional seizure. It is also necessary to show that unless an arrest is ordered, the enforcement of the claim may be endangered. It is recommended that documentary evidence be prepared to fulfil the two above requirements in time.

(2) Compulsory execution

It is necessary to show the court the full validity of a claim in the form of a court judgment, etc.

(3) Public auction without a judgment

It is necessary to show the court the validity of a claim by a mortgage certificate, vouchers, etc.

Deposit to be put up by the arrestor

A claimant needs to put up the following deposit with the court or its agency to arrest a ship. The deposit is refundable, with low interest, on some conditions, e.g. obtaining the written consent of the owner of the arrested ship, or a court decision to release the security.

(1) Provisional arrest

   (a) Cash.
   (b) Negotiable instrument, for example a company's shares, or government bonds.
   (c) Letter of guarantee issued by a bank or an insurance company (not a P. & I. Club) registered in Japan.

The court usually requires a deposit from the claimant in the event of arrest as provisional seizure, in addition to the court costs and so on, equivalent to roughly one-third to one-fifth of the amount of the claim, to cover any possible damage sustained by the owner of the ship if the arrest is later found to have been wrongful. Theoretically, the amount of security is wholly at the discretion of the court and, subject to the case, the court would offer an amount less than the above ratio.

As a deposit, cash, including a special banker's draft (cashier's cheque) issued by a commercial bank with authority given by the authorities concerned, is acceptable in its full amount. Government bonds or other reliable negotiable securities are acceptable, but they are often undervalued because of less stability. A bank guarantee or a letter of indemnity issued by an authorized bank/insurance company in Japan is also acceptable to the authorities. A letter of indemnity issued by a P. & I. Club is not acceptable for this purpose.

(2) Compulsory execution

Arrest by compulsory execution usually needs no deposit other than the nominal court costs and the like except for some certain claims, in which case a claimant needs to put up the following deposit with the court or its agency to arrest a ship:

- (a) Cash.
- (b) Negotiable instrument, for example a company's shares, or government bonds.
- (c) Letter of guarantee issued by a bank or an insurance company (not a P. & I. Club) registered in Japan.

(3) Public auction without a judgment

No deposit is necessary other than the nominal court costs and the like.

Counter-security

(1) Provisional arrest

The shipowner can obtain the release of his arrested ship by putting up a counter-security, the amount of which is fixed by the court when the order of provisional arrest has been given, that is in the maximum equal to the amount of the claim, plus interest thereon. In releasing a ship provisionally arrested, however, cash is the only counter-security.

(2) Compulsory execution

The shipowner can obtain the release of his ship arrested on the basis of a final judgment by putting up a counter-security the amount of which should be equivalent to all the claims plus the court execution costs.

The following deposit is accepted by the court to release the arrested ship:

(a) Cash.
(b) Negotiable instrument, for example a company's shares, or government bonds.
(c) Letter of guarantee issued by a bank, an insurance company or a P. & I. Club recognized in Japan.

(3) Public auction without a judgment

Same as above (2).

For a vessel arrested on the basis of maritime lien, a letter of indemnity or a letter of guarantee issued by an authorized bank, insurance company or P. & I. Club in Japan is also accepted.

NOTE

(a) In order to take steps to release the vessel, the master can statutorily represent the shipowner if the vessel is away from her registered port.
(b) Counter-security is also refundable on some conditions as referred to above.
(c) In practice, a letter of indemnity issued by a P. & I. Club, whether Japanese or foreign, or an escrow account is often accepted by the arrestor out of court, in exchange for the arrestor's withdrawal of the arrest procedure.

Authority

The District Court in the district where the vessel is berthed or at anchor is usually the competent court.

Form for application

The following clerical particulars are usually required to be filled in on the application form:

- (a) Claimant's full name and his registered (or principal) address.
- (b) When the claimant is a body corporate, the full name of one of the directors who is authorized to represent it in the litigation.
- (c) When a counsel in Japan is appointed to represent the claimant, the full name of the counsel (not merely the name of the company or law firm for which he works).
- (d) For the purpose of identification, the registered name of the vessel to be arrested (and the identification number), her material, her nationality, port of registry, gross tonnage, type and number of engines, time of her launch and the place where she is lying, as precisely as possible.
- (e) The full name of the master of the vessel and his whereabouts, if known.
- (f) The full name and the address of the registered owner of the vessel.
- (g) When the registered shipowner is a body corporate, the full name of one of the representative directors.

If a body corporate is involved on either the claimant's or the shipowner's side, certified copies of the company registration issued by the authority are usually required to accompany the application form in addition to a certified copy of the registration of the vessel.

In order to prove the existence of a foreign body corporate and of its representative director referring to his authority, whether claimant or shipowner, an affidavit prepared by the claimant's clerk or secretary or by one who reasonably knows the defendant may usually be accepted. It is recommended that the affidavit be notarized by a local Notary Public, if time permits. No authentication of such a Notary Public by the Japanese Consulate to that locality is usually necessary.

The court occasionally accepts a certified photostat copy of Lloyd's Register of Ships, Lloyd's List of Shipowners or Blue Book, listing the existence of the ship to be arrested and of her ownership. Likewise, the master's name may possibly be proved by quoting some shipping documents.

NOTE

In the court, Japanese is the only official language. Almost all the documents written in foreign languages must be translated into Japanese. No official certificate of translation is usually necessary.

Power of attorney

It is usually necessary to give counsel a written power of attorney to enable him to represent the claimant. In addition to a general authority which statutorily includes action in the arrest proceedings, some other items, if they are necessary, must be written word by word in the power of attorney, for example withdrawal of the action, compromise, appointment of sub-counsel.

The power of attorney must be executed by an individual claimant or a representative director of a body corporate and, in the case of a foreign applicant, notarization by a local Notary Public is usually required. No authentication of the authority of the Notary Public by the Japanese Consulate to the locality is now necessary.

Both the affidavit describing the existence of a body corporate and of its representative director and the power of attorney may be notarized by the same Notary Public at the same time.

If time does not permit a party to formally execute the affidavit and the power of attorney in advance, telex authorization by him or by the counsel in his country instructing a Japanese power of attorney may probably be accepted by the court. In this case, formal documentation should be submitted to the court as soon as reasonably possible.

Enforcement of the order of arrest

The claimant must go to the bailiff (executory authorities or court Marshal) and apply for enforcement of the order. It is normally sufficient to serve the order of arrest on the master, whether the vessel is Japanese or foreign. The court bailiff must take the ship's nationality certificate from the ship.

Proceedings for maintaining an arrest

(1) Provisional arrest

The court, upon application by the claimant, may nominate and order a guard to watch and preserve the arrested ship on behalf of the court so as not to allow her to physically leave the port without the court's permission.

The arrestor does not have to take further steps in principle. However, the court may, upon application by the shipowner, order the arrestor to file a substantial lawsuit in terms of the claim upon which the arrest in the form of provisional seizure was made within such a time as is fixed by the court. Should the arrestor not comply with that order, the arrest proceeding is ceased.

If the maintaining of an arrest renders some extra cost and, nevertheless, the arrestor puts up no deposit to cover it, the court may cease the effect of the arrest.

(2) Compulsory execution and (3) Public auction without a judgment

The court, upon application by the claimant, may nominate and order a guard to watch and preserve the arrested ship on behalf of the court so as not to allow her to physically leave the port without the court's permission. The costs necessary for the preservation shall be advanced by the claimant to the court.

If a Japanese flag ship has been arrested, entry of the application for the enforced ship's sale is made in the register. After such registration is made, third parties cannot effectively obtain any right on the ship which would prejudice the claimant.

Appraisal

For (2) Compulsory Execution and (3) Public Auction without a Judgment, the court shall appoint an expert, often a professional surveyor, to evaluate the ship in the process of the auction. If the court considers the valuation improper, it may order further appraisal. The minimum price is declared by the court taking into account the expert's appraisal. If no bid meets the minimum price, the court may propose a lower price as the new minimum price.

Sale

In (2) Compulsory Execution and (3) Public Auction without a Judgment proceedings, the commencement of the enforced sale proceedings is in principle notified by the court to the arrestor, registered mortgagees, registered tax authorities, etc.

The notice of the date of auction shall be given at least two weeks beforehand, and the date of the determination of the successful bidder shall be fixed within a week after the date of auction.

The sale of the arrested ship is carried out by the court Marshal (bailiff) at a public auction. The court may, however, order sale by tender instead of public auction, in which case the tendered prices are not known to the other bidders until the court Marshal has opened the sealed tenders.

Two-tenths of the offered price shall usually be deposited in cash, negotiable instrument, cashier's cheque or a bank guarantee by the bidders. The deposit is usually refundable after the successful bidder has been determined. The remaining eight-tenths of the price shall be paid in cash to the court within a certain time after the bidder has been determined by the court.

When a Japanese ship is sold through the court, the successful bidder will obtain the ownership of the ship free from any encumbrances except that the bidder must pay for a claim giving rise to the possessory lien, etc.

Proceeds of sale

In (2) Compulsory Execution and (3) Public Auction without a Judgment proceedings, the proceeds shall be distributed by the court at the date fixed by the court, at which time all creditors are heard.

The priorities between claims are summarized as follows:

1. Costs for the sale including costs for preservation and maintenance of the vessel.
2. Maritime lien.
3. Ship's mortgage.
4. National and local taxes and dues.

Appeal proceedings

(1) Provisional arrest

If the arrest as provisional seizure was granted without a hearing from the defendant, which is usually the case, the first decree to arrest a vessel by the court is not final. Upon a motion by a debtor (shipowner) a hearing is held and the same court may reverse or change the contents of the decree which becomes a decision in a more formal way. However, an application for the protest itself does not automatically stop the effect of the provisional arrest proceedings. A speedy way to release the vessel from arrest is to put up a counter-security with the Authority, leaving a dispute as to the concept of the claim to a later stage.

Thereafter an appeal within a certain number of days can be made to the High Court and, with leave, to the Supreme Court.

(2) Compulsory execution and (3) Public auction without a judgment

An objection may be made against the sale at any stage from the commencement of the enforced sale until the distribution of the proceeds becomes ready to be carried out, on the grounds of either the procedure being improper, non-existence of right of execution, etc.

However, such objection does not automatically stay the sale proceedings and the distribution of the proceeds unless the court orders a stay upon counter-security.

International Conventions

Japan has not ratified the Brussels Arrest Convention of 1952 nor the 1926 and the 1967 Conventions on Maritime Liens and Mortgages.

Difference in treatment between Japanese and foreign ships

Upon arrangement by the court an arrest of a Japanese-registered ship is to be registered in the Japanese Ships Register, while that is not the case if a foreign ship is arrested. A public ship, whether Japanese or foreign, usually cannot be the object of arrest.

As for immunity of a State-owned ship, Japan has not ratified the 1926 Convention on Immunity of State-owned Ships. According to decisions at the District Court level, a Socialist State-owned ship engaged in usual commercial activity can reportedly be arrested under certain circumstances.

Time element

(1) Provisional arrest

An arrest can usually be obtained the same day or the next day after the application is made provided the necessary evidence is available and the deposit and a bailiff are arranged in time.

(2) Compulsory execution and (3) Public auction without a judgment

An arrest itself can be carried out quickly. However, there is no definite provision for a period during which the enforced sale shall be concluded. It usually takes a few or several months from the time of the arrest of a ship until the time of the auction, subject to the circumstances.

Other particulars of interest

(a) No vessel having completed the preparations for commencing a voyage can usually be arrested unless the claimant's claim arises from the preparation for the commencement of such a voyage.

(b) If the voyage has been stopped by arrest, the court may, under certain circumstances, permit the ship to resume her voyage.

(c) As a precaution, it is recommended that the applicant for arrest notify the harbour authorities of the arrest of the ship to prevent her from sailing without authority.

In one case that we know of, a Korean-flag general cargo carrier left the port of Tokyo, where she had been arrested, without the court's permission. The port authority (Japan Maritime Safety Agency, whose function is somewhat similar to the United States Coast Guard) had been informed of the arrest. A few days after her disappearance from Tokyo the Maritime Safety Agency found her in Kanmon Strait, chased her, and eventually captured her in Tsushima Strait.

(d) An arrest of a ship does not legally affect loading or discharge of cargo on board her. If a ship has perishable cargo on board, however, her arrest will possibly cause problems with the cargo interests, ship's crew, etc., with the result that the arrest and/or the enforced sale proceedings will not proceed smoothly.

The United States

CHRISTIE HELMER

The United States court system

The legal system of the United States has two primary sets of courts which deal with maritime[1] disputes – the federal court system and the state court system. The systems are related geographically: each state has a branch of the federal system physically located in it. The systems are not related categorically: a state court lawsuit is processed entirely through the state court system, and a federal court lawsuit is processed entirely through the federal court system.

The branch of the federal court system which is located in each state is the level at which trials occur – the district court. Each of the states has one or more federal district courts. Appeals from district court decisions are taken to the federal circuit court. Each of the states belongs to one of the 11 federal circuits. The court of last resort in the federal system is the United States Supreme Court. There is only one United States Supreme Court.

The state court system is completely independent of the federal court system. Each of the 50 states has its own state trial and appellate courts. The court of last resort in the state system is each state's supreme court.

There are no special courts in either the federal or state system which were created only to hear admiralty matters. And admiralty matters are not assigned to judges with specifically maritime or even general commercial experience. In fact, if a judge who hears an admiralty case has expertise in the area, it happens merely as a matter of chance. Because admiralty law is somewhat unique, those lawyers who practice it frequently practice it exclusively or, at least, as a major part of their work. Because transportation by water is not as significant a commercial activity in the United States as some other enterprises, few lawyers learn to be admiralty lawyers. And, because judges are ordinarily selected or elected from practicing lawyers, the number of judges who have an understanding of the shipping industry or of admiralty law are relatively few.

1. In the United States, the words "maritime," "admiralty" and "marine" are used interchangeably, and they will be used that way in this chapter.

More admiralty cases are heard in the federal court system than in the state court system. Thus, an admiralty litigant's chances of obtaining a judge who understands shipping and understands admiralty law are much better in the federal court system. Of course, the geographic location of some federal district courts is much more likely to produce admiralty disputes than others (i.e., New York versus Alabama) due to the difference in quantity of significant water-related activity at the various locations of federal district courts. Those courts which frequently handle admiralty disputes are more likely to have procedures to deal smoothly with vessel arrests and attachments and are more likely to apply admiralty law on an internationally uniform basis.

Both federal and state courts have admiralty jurisdiction; that is, they have the power to decide disputes which are maritime in nature. But the jurisdiction of both systems is not the same. In some areas of maritime law (including vessel *arrest*, but not vessel *attachment*), federal court jurisdiction is exclusive.[2] The state courts have no power to hear those kinds of maritime disputes. There is no kind of maritime dispute which the federal courts do not have power to hear. Even when a maritime dispute is of such a nature that state courts have the power to adjudicate it, that does not mean that those courts have the power to apply the substantive law of their own states to resolve those disputes. Federal substantive law applies in most maritime cases, even if those cases are being tried in state courts.

Both federal and state court systems follow a hierarchical pattern. If a maritime dispute is one in which federal law applies, and the United States Supreme Court has rendered an opinion on the issue, then that opinion is law. If a maritime dispute is one in which federal law applies, but the United States Supreme Court has either not rendered an opinion or has rendered one which is subject to interpretation, the federal circuit appellate courts may differ on an issue.

Likewise, while a federal district trial court will ordinarily follow the law as its circuit appellate court has dictated, if that appellate court has not rendered an opinion on an issue, or has rendered an opinion which is subject to interpretation, federal district courts within a circuit may differ on an issue. State courts follow a similar

2. An action directly against the vessel on a maritime lien is available only in federal court. *The Moses Taylor*, 71 U.S. (4 Wall) 411 (1866); *The Hine* v. *Trevor*, 71 U.S. (4 Wall) 555 (1866).

pattern within each state, but there is no requirement in the United States legal system that the law be consistent from state to state. Thus, while there is definitive statutory and procedural law in both federal and state jurisdictions in the area of arrest and attachment, that law will differ from state to state, district to district and circuit to circuit.[3]

An individual may always represent himself in any court in the United States, but a business which operates as a corporation must be represented in court by an attorney. And no one but an attorney may represent another in court. Attorneys are licensed to practice by state and can only practice in the state and federal courts of the state where they are licensed. Each state has its own licensing examination. Thus, few attorneys practice law outside their immediate geographical region. A person wanting to arrest a vessel in Texas will likely have to find a Texas lawyer who practices admiralty law to do it.

Arrest of vessels under United States law

United States law distinguishes between *arrest* of a vessel and *attachment* of a vessel. A vessel is arrested only when a maritime lien is being foreclosed.[4] This type of lawsuit is known as an *in rem* action: the vessel is a defendant.[5] A vessel is attached when the court takes possession of it because it is property belonging to a defendant. This

3. The federal district courts use procedural rules adopted for them by the United States Supreme Court. The rules used in civil cases, including admiralty, are known as the "Federal Rules of Civil Procedure". When referred to in this chapter, those rules will be cited simply as "Rule". Additional procedural rules were adopted for the federal district courts to use in handling certain kinds of procedures thought to be uniquely maritime in nature. Those rules are known as the "Supplemental Rules for Certain Admiralty and Maritime Claims". When referred to in this chapter, those rules will be cited as "Admiralty Rule".

Each federal district court also has the power to adopt its own local rules. Those rules are used to fill in procedural gaps left by the Rules and the Admiralty Rules and to recognize local practices. The use of such local rules in admiralty litigation has been approved by case law. *The Cleona*, 37 F. 2d 599, 1930 A.M.C. 722 (S.D.N.Y. 1930).

4. A vessel is also arrested when it is seized by the United States Government because it has done something which subjects it to forfeiture or a fine. This procedure, while similar to a lien foreclosure, is not usually referred to as one. Government seizure of a vessel is outside the scope of this chapter.

5. The "defendant" is the person or entity in the lawsuit against whom the claim is being asserted. The person asserting the claim is the "plaintiff". Plaintiffs arresting a vessel used to be called "libellants" in the United States. Attorneys who practiced admiralty law were called "proctors", and lawsuits seeking arrest of a vessel were called libels. No special names are now used for admiralty procedures.

type of lawsuit is known as an *in personam* action: people (or companies) are the defendants.

What constitutes a maritime lien is defined both by statutory and case law in the United States. The kinds of claims for which United States law commonly recognizes a maritime lien against a vessel are: (1) personal injury and death caused by a vessel[6] (2) cargo damage caused by a vessel[7] (3) shore structure damage caused by a vessel[8] (4) the cost of supplies and necessary services furnished to a vessel[9] (5) vessel damage caused by collision[10] (6) preferred ship's mortgages[11] (7) seamen's and masters' wages[12] (8) salvage of a vessel[13] and (9) general average contributions by a vessel.[14] There are other less frequently encountered types of claims arising in contract (that is, dealing with agreements between parties)[15] or tort (that is, dealing with noncontractual duties between parties)[16] which also give rise to maritime liens.

A maritime lien can only be foreclosed against the object to which it relates. With tort claims, that object is the object which caused the damage (i.e., a vessel which struck a dock or on which a longshore-man was injured). With contract claims, that object is the object which the parties agree will be the subject of the lien (i.e., a vessel for which construction costs were incurred becomes the subject of a preferred ship's mortgage). This chapter focuses on maritime liens

6. See, e.g. *The Osceola*, 189 U.S. 158 (1903) (seaman's personal injuries based on unseaworthiness); *The Max Morris*, 137 U.S. 1 (1890) (longshoreman's personal injuries); *The Admiral Peoples*, 295 U.S. 649, 1935 A.M.C. 875 (1935) (passenger's personal injuries); *Moragne* v. *States Marine Lines Inc.*, 398 U.S. 375, 1970 A.M.C. 967 (1970) (death).

7. 46 U.S.C. ss.190–196 (The Harter Act) and 46 U.S.C. ss.1300–1315 (The Carriage of Goods by Sea Act).

8. 46 U.S.C. s.740 (The Admiralty Jurisdiction Extension Act).

9. 46 U.S.C. ss.971–975 (The Federal Maritime Lien Act).

10. *The China*, 74 U.S. (7 Wall) 53 (1869).

11. 46 U.S.C. s.911 (The Ship Mortgage Act).

12. *The John G. Stevens*, 170 U.S. 113 (1898) (seamen's wages) and 46 U.S.C. s.606 (wages of masters of United States' documented vessels).

13. *The Sabine*, 101 U.S. 384 (1879).

14. See, e.g. *Dupont de Nemours & Co.* v. *Vance*, 60 U.S. (19 How) 162 (1856).

15. See, e.g. *The Oceano*, 148 F. 131 (S.D.N.Y. 1906) (breach of a charter-party); *Brock* v. *S.S Southampton*, 231 F. Supp. 278 (D. Or. 1964) (advance of funds to meet payment due on preferred ship's mortgage).

16. See e.g. *Morrisey* v. *S.S. A. & J. Faith*, 252 F. Supp. 54, 1966 A.M.C. 71 (1965) (unseaworthiness as respects cargo claims); *The Henry W. Breyer*, 17 F. 2d 423, 1927 A.M.C. 290 (1927) (fraud or misrepresentation as respects cargo claims); *The Lydia*, 1 F. 2d 18, 1924 A.M.C. 1001 (2d Cir. 1924), cert. denied, 266 U.S. 616 (1924) (conversion).

against vessels, but maritime liens against other types of maritime property (i.e., cargo carried by water) also exist.[17]

Federal laws dealing with maritime disputes developed concurrently in the United States with state laws dealing with those disputes. Several states passed laws which allowed the state courts to arrest vessels and foreclose maritime liens against them. The United States Supreme Court subsequently held, however, that the jurisdiction of federal courts in the area of maritime lien foreclosure was exclusive.[18]

Maritime liens can only be foreclosed in a federal district court in the district in which a vessel to which the lien relates is found (*Johnson v. Oil Transport Co. Inc.*).[18a] As each state constitutes a different federal district, it is sometimes difficult to initiate and effect arrest procedures while a vessel in fact remains within the district. Of course, it is always possible to prepare the necessary court filings prior to the time a vessel comes into the district so the litigation can be initiated and the arrest effected immediately on the vessel being available for arrest. The necessary court filings could be made prior to the time a vessel comes into the district; however, as court filings in the United States are published in a newspaper of general circulation on the day or the following day after they are made, a pre-arrest filing would alert those with an interest in the vessel and perhaps cause the vessel to be diverted out of the district.

In order to initiate arrest of a vessel, a lawsuit must be commenced in the federal district court where the vessel will be arrested.[19] Lawsuits are commenced in both federal and state courts by filing

17. *4885 Bags of Linseed*, 66 U.S. (1 Black) 108 (1861) (cargo); *United States* v. *Freights of the S.S. Mount Shasta*, 274 U.S. 466 (1927) (freights).

18. *The Moses Taylor, supra*, at fn. 2; *The Hine* v. *Trevor, supra*, at fn. 2; *The Lottawanna*, 87 U.S. (20 Wall) 201 (1873). A number of the states still have in existence statutes which provide for foreclosure of maritime liens by vessel arrest in state courts. Only a portion of those statutes is now effective. The statutes can provide some maritime lien foreclosure procedures not inconsistent with the general federal admiralty law, can confer maritime lien status on maritime claims which are not liens under the general federal admiralty law, and can create non-maritime liens to be enforced in state court by procedures other than an *in rem* seizure. *Southern Pacific Co.* v. *Jensen*, 244 U.S. 205 (1917); *The Corsair*, 145 U.S. 335 (1892); *Edwards* v. *Elliott*, 88 U.S. (21 Wall) 532 (1874). These state laws must, however, simply be ignored to the extent that they purport to give a right to foreclose a maritime lien *in rem* in state court.

18a. 440 F. 2d 109, 1971 A.M.C. 1038 (5th Cir. 1971), cert. denied, 404 U.S. 987 (1972).

19. The Admiralty Rule which deals specifically with arrest is Rule C, and a vessel arrest in the United States is sometimes known as a "Rule C" procedure.

with the court a document called a complaint. A complaint which seeks to arrest a vessel must state that the claim being filed is based on a maritime lien and must state the circumstances giving rise to the lien, the amount of the damages suffered and the kind of relief sought (arrest of the vessel, judgment for the amount of the claim and foreclosure of the lien). The filing of this complaint should be sufficient to, at the request of plaintiff, require the federal court clerk to issue a warrant of arrest – an instruction to the United States Marshal to arrest the vessel by taking it into his possession. While complaints are ordinarily signed only by an attorney, a complaint seeking an arrest must be signed under oath, and that may require the arresting party's signature.

Before initiating the arrest, the arresting party should be certain it has the right to do that, that is, that its claim is one which gives rise to a maritime lien, that the claim is meritorious, that the vessel it seeks to arrest is the one it has the lien against, and that the judicially prescribed arrest procedures will be carefully followed. If the arrest is wrongful and was done maliciously or in bad faith, the arresting party will be liable in damages to the person entitled to possession of the vessel.[20] The Foreign Sovereign Immunities Act, 28 U.S.C. ss.1602–1611, makes property of a "foreign state" immune from arrest. To be the property of a "foreign state," a vessel need not be owned directly by a government but may be owned by a separate corporation which is, in effect, run by a foreign government.[21]

United States Supreme Court opinions which focused on the right of a consumer defendant to have an opportunity for hearing before

20. There is probably not as much risk in being held liable for wrongful seizure of property in an admiralty context as there is in other areas. Doing something wrong is not enough to create liability. You must know the arrest you are undertaking is wrongful and do it anyway. There is, of course, some danger that failing to make a reasonable effort to determine if an arrest is well founded can amount to "knowledge". Damages for wrongful arrest can include the cost of any release bond, attorneys' fees incurred in defending against arrest, extra wharfage and similar extra seizure expenses, and operating costs. Profits lost because the detention prevented the vessel from undertaking a new charter have been held not to be recoverable, but other real losses incurred by the vessel owner are recoverable (i.e. a penalty paid for failure to deliver a vessel under charter or loss of charter hire). *Ocean Ship Supply* v. *Leah*, 729 F. 2d 971, 1984 A.M.C. 2089 (4th Cir. 1984); *Frontera Fruit Company* v. *Dowling*, 91 F. 2d 293, 1937 A.M.C. 1259 (5th Cir. 1937); *TTT Stevedores of Tex. Inc.* v. *M/V Jagat Vijeta*, 509 F. Supp. 1072, 1981 A.M.C. 2446 (E.D. Tex. 1981); *Techem Chemical Co. Ltd.* v. *MT Choyo Maru*, 416 F. Supp. 960, 1976 A.M.C. 1954 (D. Md. 1976).

21. *O'Connell Machinery Company, Inc.* v. *M/V Americana*, 734 F. 2d 115 (2nd Cir. 1984); *Sumler* v. *South African Marine*, 1983 A.M.C. 1878 (E.D. Va. 1982); *Complaint of Rio Grande Transport Inc.*, 516 F. Supp. 1155 (D.C. N.Y. 1981).

certain of his property was taken[22] have been expanded by some
districts to apply to foreclosure of a maritime lien by arrest of a
vessel.[23] These districts will require a court order authorizing the
issuance of a warrant for arrest before the clerk will issue a warrant
and before the Marshal will act on the warrant.

In a district where a court order is required to effect an arrest, after
or contemporaneous with the filing of the complaint, a motion (that
is, a request for court action) asking for an arrest must be filed. The
district may require the motion to be accompanied by an affidavit or
other form of sworn testimony discussing the circumstances giving
rise to the right of arrest. Because vessel arrests are usually urgent
business, a prompt hearing before a federal district court can
ordinarily be obtained without the necessity of waiting until the
motion comes on for hearing on the court's regular docket. No notice
to anyone of the court hearing on such a motion is ordinarily
required.[24] If there is no suspicion that the vessel against which arrest
is sought will try to escape, an attorney may, as a matter of courtesy,
notify the attorney representing the vessel (if known) of any hearing
time on the motion for arrest.

The court has the power to require the arresting party to post a
bond for any costs and expenses that might be awarded against it
should the lawsuit initiating the arrest be successfully defended. No
bond is ordinarily required. The Marshal usually requires, however,
that cash be posted to pay his fees before he will act on an arrest

22. *Fuentes* v. *Shevin*, 407 U.S. 67 (1972); *Sniadach* v. *Family Finance Corp.*, 395 U.S. 337
(1969).

23. See, e.g. *Alyeska Pipeline Service Co.* v. *The Vessel Bay Ridge*, 509 F. Supp. 1115 (D.
Alaska 1981); *Karl Senner Inc.* v. *M/V Acadian Valor*, 485 F. Supp. 287 (Ed. La. 1980).
This is a rapidly developing area of law in the United States, and particular attention
should be paid at the time of an arrest to the status of this area of the law in the district
where the arrest is contemplated.
Cases in most districts have held that Rule C arrests are sufficiently different from
other kinds of prejudgment property seizures to avoid the effect of *Sniadach* and *Fuentes*.
See, e.g. *Amstar Corp.* v. *S.S. Alexandros T.*, 664 F. 2d 904 (4th Cir. 1981); *Merchants
National Bank* v. *Dredge General G. L. Gillespie*, 663 F. 2d 1338 (5th Cir. 1981); *Kodiak
Fishing Company* v. *M/V Pacific Pride*, 535 F. Supp. 915 (D. Wash. 1982); *Inter-American
Shipping Enterprise Ltd.* v. *The Tula*, 1982 A.M.C. 951 (Ed. Va. 1981); *United States* v.
Kaiyo Maru No. 53, 503 F. Supp. 1075 (D. Alaska 1980); *Hjalmar Bjorges Rederi* v. *The
Tugboat Condor*, 1979 A.M.C. 1696 (S.D. Cal. 1979); *Amoco Overseas Oil Co.* v. *Compagnie
Nationale Alterienne*, 459 F. Supp. 1242 (S.D.N.Y. 1978), aff'd 605 F. 2d 648 (2d Cir.
1979); *Central Soya Co.* v. *Cox Towing Corp.*, 417 F. Supp. 658 (N.D. Miss. 1976);
Bethlehem Steel Corp. v. *S/T Valiant King*, 1977 A.M.C. 1919 (Ed. Pa. 1974).

24. Whether a potential defendant is entitled to a preseizure hearing is the issue that
cases considering the viability of a Rule C arrest focus on.

warrant. United States law allows Marshals to request payment in advance of a reasonable amount towards their arrest and custody expenses. Advances of $1,000–$10,000 are commonly requested.

The arresting party's involvement in the arrest does not end when a warrant for arrest is secured and delivered to the Marshal. It is not the Marshal's job to find the vessel sought to be arrested. The Marshal must be specifically instructed on the whereabouts of the vessel. If the Marshal cannot drive to the vessel because it is at anchor or is navigating, the party seeking arrest must provide the Marshal with the means to board the vessel; that is, he must hire a launch or a helicopter or must persuade the local pilots or members of the United States Coast Guard to assist the Marshal in boarding the vessel. Once the Marshal has boarded the vessel and posted a copy of the arrest warrant in some prominent location, he has it in his custody as a representative of the court. The vessel cannot leave without obtaining a court order[25] authorizing its release from custody.

Only a federal district court Marshal can arrest a vessel,[26] but any responsible, bonded person familiar with vessels can take custody of a vessel after arrest and hold the vessel until it is released by the court. These people, called "substitute custodians," must be appointed by court order and approved by the Marshal for each case in which they serve. Substitute custodians are used because their custodial fees are significantly less than those of the Marshal and because, in many districts, there is an insufficient number of Marshals to handle the custody and care of arrested vessels. In some districts, so few Marshals are available that an arrest will not be made until a substitute custodian has been appointed. The substitute custodian must be provided by the arresting party, and court personnel are not ordinarily familiar with the names of qualified substitute custodians.

The Marshal or substitute custodian does not take an active role in managing the vessel once it is arrested. In fact, oftentimes the Marshal or substitute custodian does not even stay aboard the vessel.

---

25. Admiralty Rule E(5)(c) actually allows a vessel to be released by the court clerk on stipulation of the parties, but in almost all districts, either by local rule or in practice, the federal court clerk will not exercise that authority and the Marshal will not recognize a release which is not a court order. Other actions which this chapter refers to as requiring a court order may sometimes actually be done by the clerk or Marshal if they were willing to exercise the full extent of their authority. Often times, however, the parties want a court order as evidence that they were allowed to take action the way they did.

26. Admiralty Rule C(3).

The arrest may be physically accomplished, and the right to possession of the vessel placed in the Marshal, simply by the Marshal's tacking a copy of the arrest warrant in a conspicuous place on the vessel and leaving a copy of the complaint and arrest warrant with the person in charge of the vessel (Admiralty Rule E(4)(b)). If there is no reason to believe a vessel will try to escape, the Marshal or custodian will sit in a car or trailer near the vessel or will simply check on the vessel at appropriate intervals. The Marshal can notify Customs officials of a vessel's arrest and cause the vessel's clearance to be withheld until it has been released from arrest (Admiralty Rule E(4)(b)).

A vessel need not be kept inactive while arrested. A court order may ordinarily be obtained to allow the vessel to load or unload cargo or to shift berths. The only custodial requirement which the court does not have the power to change is the requirement that the vessel remain within the technical boundaries of the federal court district[27] and that the Marshal or substitute custodian retain ultimate responsibility for the vessel.

Where the vessel will physically remain throughout pendency of the arrest is the responsibility of the arresting party. Arrested vessels are not kept in any designated place, and neither the court nor the Marshal will ordinarily assist an arresting party in selecting a suitable moorage. The arresting party assumes responsibility for moorage fees as well as the fees of the Marshal or substitute custodian, and moorage fees may also be required in advance if the vessel is expected to be under arrest for any length of time. Sometimes an anchorage position is available without charge.

A person having an interest in the arrested vessel can obtain its release at any time subsequent to arrest and before sale by successfully contending that the arrest is wrongful or by posting a bond to stand as security in lieu of the vessel (Admiralty Rule E(5)). On request of such a person, a court hearing must be held to litigate the propriety of the arrest, determine the amount of any bond, or approve the amount of any bond agreed to between the arresting party and the party seeking release. While the scheduling of such a hearing must of

27. In order for a court to retain *in rem* jurisdiction over a vessel (that is, retain the power to affect ownership and possession of the vessel), the vessel or some form of security posted in lieu of it must remain in the district. *L. B. Harvey Marine Inc.* v. *M/V River Arc*, 712 F. 2d 458 (11th Cir. 1983); *Bank of Wage Claims* v. *Registry of the District Court of Guam*, 431 F. 2d 1215, 1971 A.M.C. 1298 (9th Cir. 1970); *Martin* v. *The Bud*, 172 F. 2d 295, 1949 A.M.C. 544 (9th Cir. 1949); *Diners/Fugazy Sales Corp.* v. *S.S. Cariba*, 302 F. Supp. 406, 1969 A.M.C. 1591 (E.D.N.Y. 1969).

necessity depend on the availability of a judge to hear the matter, most federal district courts recognize the revenue lost by keeping an arrested vessel in custody and will accommodate the parties involved by scheduling an immediate or early hearing.

The amount of bond which is normally required to obtain release of an arrested vessel is an amount large enough to cover the full amount of the claim of the arresting party, including any attorneys' fees to which the party would be entitled, prejudgment interest and costs of arresting and keeping the vessel. A bond may be in the form of cash, an undertaking by certain recognized surety companies, or whatever form of security or promise is acceptable to the arresting party. The arresting party should be certain, however, before the vessel is released, that the security accepted in lieu of the vessel is adequate to cover all of the plaintiff's potential claim. If a plaintiff's claim when proved exceeds the amount of the security, or if the security depreciates in value (i.e. a surety company fails or a cash bond is poorly invested) by the time the plaintiff obtains a judgment, United States law may not allow the plaintiff to rearrest the vessel.[28] There is not now a United States Supreme Court opinion on this issue, and whether rearrest will be allowed depends on what federal district court the plaintiff is in.

If the vessel owner or someone having an interest in the vessel (i.e. a charterer) disputes the validity or amount of the lien asserted by the arresting party, that dispute is raised by the party filing a claim to the vessel in the pending lawsuit.[29] The case initiated by the complaint will then proceed to trial like any other lawsuit in the United States.[30]

Initiating the lawsuit does expose the arresting party to a little known risk. Admiralty Rule E(7) provides that, where a party defending against an arrest has given security for the arresting party's claim and has asserted a counterclaim (that is, a claim against the plaintiff arresting party), the arresting party must put up security for the defending party's claim in order to proceed with the lawsuit. In the United States, security is ordinarily required to be posted for a pending claim only when the claim is in a definite amount (i.e. a claim

28. See e.g. *Industria Nacional Del Papel, CA.* v. *M/V Albert F,* 730 F. 2d 622 (11th Cir. 1984); *Southern Oregon* v. *Sweet Pea,* 1977 A.M.C. 638 (D. Or. 1977).

29. The owner or other person claiming an interest in the vessel can enter the lawsuit for the limited purpose of contesting the arresting party's claim, and the arresting party or others joining in the lawsuit will not be able to assert other claims against him.

30. How the parties learn about each other's positions and try the case is outside the scope of this chapter. Those procedures are covered by the Rules.

on a loan of money or a sale of goods at a specified price) and there is no likelihood that the claim is defensible. Admiralty Rule E(7) does not limit its security requirement to these or any other particular kind of case. Thus, by arresting a vessel, a plaintiff exposes itself to the risk that it will be required to put up security for a claim where it would not otherwise be required to. There is some question about whether an arresting party can be required to post more in security than it has required the defending party to post.[31]

If, within 10 days after an arrest is effected, no one steps forward to seek release of the vessel, the arresting party must publish notice of the arrest in a newspaper of general circulation in the district where the vessel was arrested (Admiralty Rule C(4)). Notice is required because, if the vessel is not released, it will be sold by the court to satisfy the arresting party's claim, and all claims to or liens on the vessel will be extinguished by that judicial sale in order to give the purchaser free and clear title to the vessel.[32] Anyone claiming a lien on the vessel must intervene in the lawsuit and assert that lien, or the lien will be lost.[33]

If no one appears to seek release of the vessel or contest the arresting party's lien claim within a certain specified period of time, on motion of the arresting party, a court will enter a judgment by default on the arresting party's claim and the vessel will be sold by the Marshal to satisfy that claim (Admiralty Rule C(6); Rules 55 and 69). If a party having an interest in the vessel appears to contest the arresting party's claim, but does not seek release of the vessel, the arresting party or the Marshal may seek to have the vessel sold prior to any adjudication of the plaintiff's claim. This kind of sale is called an interlocutory sale (Admiralty Rule E(9)(b)).

It is assumed that continued judicial custody of a vessel wastes an important commercial asset and that society would be better served by sale of the vessel and retention of the proceeds to satisfy any claim which the arresting party is able to prove. This policy underlies Admiralty Rule E(9)(b). Because most vessels are released within a reasonable period after their arrest, the importance to the United States legal system of prompt sales of vessels has not been frequently

31. *Spriggs* v. *Hoffstot*, 240 F. 2d 76 (4th Cir. 1957).
32. The sale of a vessel by the Marshal in an *in rem* proceeding extinguishes all liens and all rights of any persons in the vessel. *Point Landing Inc.* v. *Alabama Dry Dock & Shipbuilding Co.* 261 F. 2d 861, 1959 A.M.C. 148 (5th Cir. 1968).
33. How to intervene is governed by Rules 19 and 20.

tested. It would seem that, in this age where vessels are not a scarce
commodity, a policy favoring interlocutory sales is no longer
appropriate. Because the policy exists, however, and because the
costs of keeping a vessel during an arrest period may themselves begin
to outweigh the value of the vessel, a party having an interest in an
arrested vessel but no immediate use for it may find its vessel sold
before it has an opportunity to prove the plaintiff's claim is without
merit.

How a vessel sale is actually set up and conducted differs from
district to district. While the Rules provide certain general sales
procedures for property which would be applicable to vessels, usually
local district court rules specifically deal with vessel sales or the court
orders a vessel sale to be held according to recognized local custom.

Procedures for preparing for the sale and handling it are set forth in
a court order authorizing the sale.[34] As with any court order, someone
must request the court to take action in the form of an order, and that
request is made by motion. The motion requesting sale would
ordinarily be made by the arresting party who wants the vessel sold so
it can receive the funds it is entitled to, but it might also be made by
the Marshal who wants to be relieved of the duty of care of the
vessel.

Notice of the sale will be given to prospective purchasers by
advertisement in one or more newspapers of general circulation.
Little in the way of publication is usually required. Court ordered
advertising may range from the publication of notice for three
consecutive days to once a week for four consecutive weeks. If there
has been a recent appraisal of the seized vessel (i.e. by a mortgagee
who has checked on the value of its security), the court may use that
appraisal to set a minimum bid price for the sale. Otherwise, the court
may order from one to three independent appraisals of the vessel to
give it a basis for determining what price must be obtained for the
vessel to make the sale a fair one. The appraisals will undoubtedly be
on a liquidation basis. The appraisals, however, are merely a
guideline for the court. If a sale of the vessel cannot be made at the
appraised price, the vessel can, and will, be allowed to be sold at
whatever price it can bring. It is very difficult to persuade a court

---

34. The order ordinarily must be strictly followed in order for the sale to be effective.
The Nancy II, 38 F. 2d 182 (1st Cir. 1930).

ordering the sale, or an appellate court reviewing that lower court's actions, that the price obtained at the sale was too low.[35]

The court sales order usually specifies how much of the bid price must be tendered at the time of the sale in order for the bid to be accepted. Ten per cent of the bid price is a common deposit requirement. The order should also specify how many days the bidder has to tender the remainder of the bid price. Both the deposit and the balance of the sales price are usually required to be in cash or certified check.

Local rules or custom usually require judicial sale of a vessel to be confirmed. This affords an opportunity to complain about the adequacy of the sales price, the adequacy of advertisements or other aspects of the sale. The court sales order will likely prescribe a waiting period before the sale will be considered final and the successful purchaser allowed to exchange the balance of the purchase price for possession of the vessel. During this period objections to the sale may be made to the court. While the court has the power to decide itself not to confirm the sale (i.e. if there were so few bidders present that the court questions whether a differently handled sale might produce a better sales price), ordinarily, if no objection is received, the sale will be ordered confirmed at the conclusion of the waiting period. Once the order confirming sale has been entered, the sale is final and cannot be set aside. Of course, an appeal can always be taken from a final order of the district court.

An order distributing the sales proceeds must be obtained before the clerk of court, with whom the proceeds are deposited, will release them to the arresting party. That order will list, in order of priority, to whom the proceeds will be distributed. Proceeds will only be distributed to the arresting party, the person claiming ownership or possession of the vessel or someone who has "intervened" in the lawsuit (that is, asked to become a party to the lawsuit to assert a claim and been granted permission by the court). If the parties cannot agree among themselves on the order of priority of their claims, a court hearing will be held to determine priority.

35. Sometimes an "upset" bid is received after the sale. An "upset" bid is one which is higher than the successful high bid at the sale. Even the receipt of a later higher bid is ordinarily insufficient to cause the court to set aside a sale. What the court looks at in reviewing a bid price is whether the bid is so grossly inadequate that it would be fraudulent or manifestly unfair to accept that bid. *Munro Drydock Inc.* v. *M/V Heron*, 585 F. 2d 13 (9th Cir. 1978); *Ghezzi* v. *Foss Launch and Tug Company*, 321 F. 2d 421 (9th Cir. 1963).

The court clerk has authority, on request of a party and an appropriate court order, to invest sales proceeds as agreed or ordered until their distribution is ordered. Investment of proceeds is frequently requested where there is an unresolved dispute as to priority of lien claims.

Attachment of vessels under United States law

"Attachment" is the court's bringing into its possession the property of a defendant when that defendant is not the property itself.[36] Both federal and state courts have the power of attachment. There are three bases for attachment in the United States:

(1) To acquire jurisdiction (that is, the power to affect) over a prospective defendant.

(2) To obtain security for satisfaction of a claim, should judgment be favorably rendered.

(3) To seize property to apply in satisfaction of a judgment.

While the concept of arrest is uniquely maritime under United States law, the concept of attachment is not. Attachment is available on almost all kinds of claims and for almost all kinds of property. The first basis for attachment, however, has acquired a distinctly maritime connotation because its use in other contexts has been limited[37] and because the power to use it is most frequently exercised by the federal court system acting under its Admiralty Rules rather than the state court system.[38]

There is probably more risk to the admiralty claimant in effecting an improper attachment than an improper arrest, as the propriety of the attachment may be governed by stricter state laws instead of the

36. If the defendant were the property itself, the action would be an "arrest".

37. The United States Supreme Court in *Shaffer* v. *Heitner*, 433 U.S. 186 (1977) decided that courts in the United States could not acquire jurisdiction over a person simply because the person had property within a court's jurisdiction. According to *Shaffer*, to do that would violate the constitutional protection afforded persons in the United States that their property would not be taken without "due process of law", that is, without their having an opportunity to be heard. As a result of this and decisions applying *Sniadach* and *Fuentes* in a maritime context, procedures for maritime attachment in the United States have been modified in recent years.

38. This form of attachment is what is commonly known as a "maritime" or "Rule B" attachment under the Admiralty Rules. The jurisdiction acquired under this form of attachment is sometimes known as *quasi in rem* jurisdiction because it is very similar to an *in rem* proceeding against the property itself.

maritime standard of malice or bad faith. Before effecting an attachment, the claimant should be certain that it has a good claim, that the property belongs to the prospective defendant and that the judicially prescribed attachment procedures are carefully followed.

Maritime attachment is used to acquire jurisdiction over a prospective defendant when the defendant does not have a sufficient presence in the territory over which the court can exercise its power to allow the court to render a judgment against it. If the prospective defendant cannot be found, by attaching its property the court can in practical terms require the defendant to come into its territory of power in order to claim its property. If the defendant fails to appear to contest the attaching plaintiff's claim, the attaching plaintiff obtains whatever portion of the attached property is necessary to satisfy its claim. If the defendant property owner does appear, he can do so for the limited purpose of defending the attaching plaintiff's claim in order to protect his property interest, and the court cannot exercise its power over him for any other reason (Admiralty Rule E(8)).

The federal courts differ widely from district to district in how much "presence" will be sufficient to find that a prospective defendant is in fact present in the jurisdiction and thus his property not subject to attachment. In at least one district, just the fact that one of the defendant's vessels happens to be in the district[39] is sufficient presence to avoid an attachment. In other districts, a foreign shipowner's vessels must make regular calls in the district before the shipowner will be deemed to have sufficient presence in the district so that no attachment of his vessels can be made.[40]

Because maritime attachment can be used only when the prospective defendant cannot be found within the state where the federal district court exerts its power, a prospective defendant could easily avoid attachment of its property by agreeing to allow the court to

39. This is the rule in the district of Oregon as a result of a state procedural rule [Oregon Rule of Civil Procedure 7D.(3)(g)] delineating how a complaint may be served on certain vessel interests. The enforceability of this rule as it applies to vessel attachments under federal law has not been tested in the courts.

This rule is, in a sense, illogical because the presence is purely transitory, and the policy behind maritime attachment is to provide security when a defendant does not otherwise have assets in the jurisdiction.

40. This is another area of rapidly developing law in the United States where the law may be applied differently from district to district. See e.g. *Cobelfret-Cie. Belge* v. *Samick Lines Co.*, 542 F. Supp. 29 (W.D. Wash. 1982); *Metal Transport Corp.* v. *Canadian Transport Co.*, 526 F. Supp. 234 (S.D.N.Y. 1981); *Integrated Container Service Inc.* v. *Starlines Container Shipping Ltd.*, 476 F. Supp. 119 (S.D.N.Y. 1979); *Andros Compania Maritima S.A.* v. *Andre & Cie. S.A.*, 430 F. Supp. 88 (S.D.N.Y. 1977).

exert its power over him. For example, if a foreign shipowner has no assets in the United States other than the vessels he rarely brings into that country, it has been held that a person acquiring a maritime attachment over one of those vessels must release the vessel from attachment if the foreign shipowner agrees that any judgment obtained against him will be a valid judgment.[41] The plaintiff may then obtain a judgment, but there will be no assets in the United States for the plaintiff to apply toward satisfaction of that judgment, and assets of the foreign shipowner in other countries may be very difficult and expensive to locate. This basis for avoiding an attachment is more often applied where the attachment has not yet been effected, but it would seem that there is little logic for distinguishing the effect of an appearance on that basis.

Because maritime or jurisdictional attachment can so easily be thwarted, the second basis for attachment – to obtain security for satisfaction of any judgment obtained – is increasingly being used when it is available. The federal court system does not have procedural rules for this form of attachment, but each federal district court has adopted the state court attachment rules for the state in which the district is located (Rule 64). These rules were not adopted specifically to deal with maritime disputes, and they sometimes do not fit well in a maritime context. Their application is improved, however, by using them in the federal court system, which is accustomed to dealing with maritime property. Thus, although this security attachment procedure could be accomplished through either the federal or state courts,[42] maritime attorneys customarily use the federal court system.

When attaching a vessel on either the first (maritime or jurisdictional attachment) or the second (attachment for security) basis, the attaching plaintiff must ordinarily arrange a court hearing to obtain a court order. Depending on local court rules, this hearing may be without notice to the prospective defendant so long as that defendant is afforded an immediate opportunity for a post-seizure hearing.[43] As

41. *Pacific Hawaiian Lines* v. *Ol Mar Inc.*, 1983 A.M.C. 2347 (W.D. Wash. 1981).

42. Where an attachment might not be effected under federal law due to the "presence" of the defendant under the law of that federal district, it may be, however, that an attachment is still possible in state court under state attachment procedures. *Gahr Development Inc. of Panama* v. *Nedlloyd Lijen B.V.*, 542 F. Supp. 1224 (E.D. La. 1982).

43. This is the area of admiralty law that has been most affected by the *Sniadach* and *Fuentes* decisions. A number of courts have considered whether, in light of those decisions, a Rule B attachment is constitutionally defective and, thus, an invalid procedure. The case-law is becoming well settled that Rule B attachments can be

with an arrest, the courts are usually willing to hear motions for attachment orders as soon as they are filed. The hearing can be held without notice to the defendant in either type of attachment, but the attachment for security requires a special showing that the giving of notice would likely mean loss of the property. To provide a basis for the court's granting an order authorizing attachment, the attaching plaintiff must, like the arresting plaintiff, file a complaint outlining the basis for its claim, the amount of damages it suffered, and the specific relief it seeks (that is, attachment of the property, judgment for the amount of damages sought, and a sale of the attached property to satisfy the judgment). A motion asking for the order and sworn affidavits supporting the plaintiff's right to the order must also be filed.

An attachment to obtain security is available in more limited circumstances than a jurisdictional attachment, and the procedures for obtaining it are more complicated. While the requirements which the court imposes on a plaintiff seeking an order authorizing a security attachment do differ from state to state, the most significant requirements are:

(1) The claim must be a liquidated claim to which the attaching plaintiff anticipates there will be no defense (i.e. a claim for charter hire or providing stevedoring services rather than a seaman's claim for personal injury).

(2) The attaching plaintiff himself (rather than his attorney) must present considerable facts to the court in the form of sworn testimony, by affidavit or otherwise, to convince the court that this is the sort of claim where security should be obtained prior to judgment.

---

permissible only when supported by appropriate local court rules or recognized local customs providing certain safeguards for the prospective defendant. *Trans-asiatic Oil* v. *Apex Oil*, 743 F. 2d 956, 1985 A.M.C. 1 (1st Cir. 1984); *Schiffartsgesellschaft* v. *A. Bottacchi*, 732 F. 2d 1543 (11th Cir. 1984); *Polar Shipping Ltd.* v. *Oriental Shipping Corp.*, 680 F. 2d 627 (9th Cir. 1982); *Intern. Ocean Way* v. *Hyde Park Navigation*, 555 F. Supp. 1047 (S.D.N.Y. 1983); *Crysen Shipping Co.* v. *Bona Shipping Co. Ltd.*, 1983 A.M.C. 237 (M.D. Fla. 1982); *Inter-American Shipping Enterprise Ltd.* v. *Tula, supra*; *Anti Costi Shipping Corp.* v. *Golar Martins*, 1980 A.M.C. 2508 (S.D.N.Y. 1979); *Grand Bahama Petroleum* v. *Canadian Transport Agencies*, 450 F. Supp. 447 (W.D. Wash. 1978); *Engineering Equipment Co.* v. *S.S. Selene*, 466 F. Supp. 706, 1978 A.M.C. 809 (S.D.N.Y. 1978); *Cooke Industries Inc.* v. *Tokyo Marine Co.*, 1978 A.M.C. 1979 (D. Alaska 1978). This is another rapidly developing area of case-law in the United States where the law will differ from district to district.

(3) A bond must be posted in an amount to be set by the court, which can be as high as twice the value of the property to be attached.

If the order authorizing attachment is granted, the court clerk issues a writ of attachment (which is the counterpart to a warrant for arrest) to the federal Marshal (or if it is a state court, the state Sheriff). The actual attachment, and the handling of the vessel itself and the parties' dispute subsequent to the attachment, are managed in the same manner as they would be were the vessel being arrested. The circumstances which prompt an interlocutory sale in the federal court of an arrested vessel will likely prompt a prejudgment sale of an attached vessel in either a federal or state court. While the specifics of prejudgment attachment sale procedures in either state or federal court will depend on the particular state,[44] they will involve the same issues as are treated in federal court sales of arrested vessels.

The United States legal system's concern, on any attachment which is obtained prior to judgment, is that the interests of the prospective defendant who may, on trial of the case, be found not to have any liability to the attaching plaintiff, be protected. As the liability of the prospective defendant has not been adjudicated, the plaintiff should not be allowed to capriciously take control of the property of another. That protection is not necessary once a judgment has been obtained. Thus, when a plaintiff is seeking to attach a vessel pursuant to a valid judgment, the procedures are dramatically simplified. No court order need be obtained. No showing of special circumstances need be made. A bond may not be required. The federal district court or state court clerk will issue a writ of attachment (sometimes also called a writ of execution or writ of garnishment) on request of any plaintiff who has a judgment entered in the court which that clerk serves, and the Marshal or Sheriff will attach the property and promptly sell it.

United States federal and state courts recognize judgments of courts other than themselves. For example, if a plaintiff obtained a judgment in the United States District Court for the District of New York, that judgment could be filed in the United States District Court

44. Because federal court attachment is accomplished pursuant to Rule 64 under the rules of the state in which the federal court is located, and because sales of court held property are to some extent accomplished in the federal courts pursuant to those state court rules, the federal courts will likely look to the procedures of the state in which they sit for the handling of prejudgment attachment sales.

for the District of Oregon, and, after the lawsuit was assigned an Oregon federal court number, the Oregon federal district court would recognize that New York federal district court judgment just as if the judgment had been obtained in the Oregon federal district court.[45] Similar simple procedures are also available in registering federal court judgments in state courts and vice versa.[46]

United States federal and state courts also recognize judgments of foreign countries (when those countries afford what is basically considered a " 'fair trial' in the United States") and awards of foreign or domestic arbitral tribunals.[47] While the proof of those judgments or awards is not as simplified a procedure as the proof of a judgment obtained in another United States court, it is nonetheless a process which takes very little time and very little in the way of evidence. Once a foreign country judgment or award becomes a United States judgment, the judgment creditor may take advantage of the post-judgment attachment procedures without meeting the requirements for a maritime jurisdictional attachment or attachment for security.

45. 28 U.S.C. s.1963.
46. See e.g. 28 U.S.C. s.1738.
47. See e.g. 9 U.S.C. ss.201–208 (foreign arbitral awards).